TRUE CRIME :
OHIO

TRUE CRIME: OHIO

The State's Most Notorious Criminal Cases

Patricia A. Martinelli

STACKPOLE
BOOKS

Published by
STACKPOLE BOOKS
5067 Ritter Road
Mechanicsburg, PA 17055
www.stackpolebooks.com

Printed in the United States of America

10 9 8 7 6 5 4 3 2 1

FIRST EDITION

Cover design by Tessa J. Sweigert

Cover photos: Edward A. Andrassy, Eliot Ness, and Cleveland Police raiding an illegal distillery during Prohibition, Cleveland Police Historical Society & Museum

Library of Congress Cataloging-in-Publication Data

Martinelli, Patricia A.
    True crime, Ohio : the state's most notorious criminal cases / Patricia A. Martinelli. — 1st ed.
        p. cm.
    Includes bibliographical references.
    ISBN-13: 978-0-8117-0650-6 (pbk.)
    ISBN-10: 0-8117-0650-8 (pbk.)
        1. Crime—Ohio—Case studies. 2. Criminals—Ohio—Case studies. I. Title.
HV6793.O3M37   2011
364.1092'2771—dc22
                                2010035399

To Jim Loretta,
my t'ai chi instructor, a born teacher
who helped inspire me to find my true path

Contents

Introduction

States, like people, are often stereotyped according to certain images. Mention New York, and many people think of the bright lights of Times Square in the Big Apple. Say the name California, and nine times out of ten, the response will be the flash and glamour of Hollywood. Once upon a time, the mention of Ohio might have called to mind endless rows of corn and placid cows grazing in grassy fields. These days, a lot of people think first of the Rock and Roll Hall of Fame and Museum in the bustling city of Cleveland, but that's just a small part of the bigger picture.

Like most of America, the Buckeye State is a region of contrasts. It has densely populated cities with close to one million residents and tiny rural towns often inhabited by less than two hundred people. Ohio has a diverse population that includes people of German, Irish, English, Polish, Italian, African, and Native American ancestry. Filled with plateaus, rivers, and open plains, the fifth most densely populated state in the union is rich with history, culture, the arts, and industry. In 2008, more than fifty of the top one thousand companies in the United States were headquartered there, including Goodyear Tire & Rubber, Abercrombie & Fitch, Procter & Gamble, and Wendy's. But lurking just behind the bright lights of Ohio's busy urban areas and sun-drenched acres of bucolic countryside is a shadowy world of crime. Robbery, rape, organized crime, and murder have become a part of life for residents of the state, just as they have for Americans everywhere. Over the years, some incidents have received national and even international attention, while most others remained little more than entries in the files of their local police departments.

Some criminologists and psychologists have dedicated themselves to analyzing the reasons why people commit crimes. They ask, did one perpetrator become a sexual predator because of a history of poverty and abuse? Did drug use turn another to a life of crime? It is unlikely, however, that we will know the answer to such questions any time soon. Every individual responds in a different way to his or her life situations. What might cause one person to become a murderer or thief might encourage another to become a teacher or a professional athlete. With all of the advances in forensic science, it's hard to believe that anyone would voluntarily break the law these days. As we are bombarded day and night with such stories in the news, there are people who wonder if evil is literally walking the earth. It's difficult not to believe such a concept when there are criminals among us who seem to have an obsessive need to do nothing else but cause trouble and pain for others.

This book does not attempt to resolve these issues that have been debated by the experts for generations. Instead, it focuses on some of the major contemporary criminal cases that have occurred in Ohio between the early years of the twentieth century and present day. The reader will be offered a selection of some of state's most famous criminal cases, which range from murder and assault to the activities of organized crime. This book will not review political corruption at length, because that's a subject that could easily fill a book of its own. It will include a look at some of the lesser-known laws that, fortunately, are rarely enforced these days. Neither will the book examine minor criminal violations, acts of civil disobedience, or ethical dilemmas. As I did with *True Crime: New Jersey*, the first book in this series, I will provide the reader with brief outlines of lesser-known cases in between more detailed accounts of specific crimes. The final chapter looks at the world of men and women who have chosen careers on the front lines of law enforcement.

Although Native Americans lived in the region long before European immigrants, their records were primarily oral, not written, so crimes and other such incidents were difficult to document. As a result, I have focused the first chapter of this book on the years after the settlers arrived. This brief history of crime between the seventeenth and nineteenth centuries will provide the reader with a better perspective on modern-day incidents. Many of us feel overwhelmed by the constant barrage of bad news that we hear on television. While it might seem like there is more criminal activity these days, that's really not true. There are just a lot more people around, so the number of crimes has increased accordingly. The reader will discover that while most people settled in Ohio with the hope of working toward a better life, a handful of others were determined to take what they could get by any means necessary. In that respect, little has changed over the years.

CHAPTER 1

A Brief History of
Crime in Ohio

Thousands of years before European immigrants flocked to the East Coast of America, native peoples lived in the region that would later become known as the state of Ohio. Today, little remains of early Indian cultures like the Plano beyond a few arrowheads, some potsherds, and a scattering of brittle skeleton fragments. Later cultures, like the Adena, who inhabited the area around 800 BCE, were believed to have lived a more settled lifestyle in the region. While they built many burial mounds, including the Great Serpent Mound in Adams County, that provide some clues to their customs, their records, like those of their predecessors, were traditionally oral. As a result, very little information was available on the types of crimes they might have committed.

It is more than likely, however, that murder, adultery, theft, and any other misdemeanors would have met with swift retribution meted out by tribal leaders or by other tribes. Exchanges between the Native Americans and the European settlers who arrived in the region were usually marked by violence and brutality, a pattern that would regularly repeat itself in the years that followed. Unlike the tribes along the East Coast, those who lived in the Ohio region often did not welcome the new arrivals.

When European colonists first arrived in America in the seventeenth century, they were amazed by the wide-open acres and apparently limitless natural resources of the New World that were available for the taking. For many of them, it was the chance to achieve opportunities that were not available in their native countries, where the aristocracy maintained a stranglehold on the land and the social order. As word traveled back to their different homelands, the eastern shores were soon filled with newcomers who crowded into cities or sought out farmland. With the population of the New World rapidly expanding, a small number of immigrants decided to push further west to the as-yet-unspoiled territories. Having survived the arduous journey from the Old World in tiny wooden sailing ships, they were unfazed by the idea of traveling by horse and wagon through hundreds of miles of mountains.

At roughly the same time, French explorers from Canada decided to travel south in search of a way to get to China. The Iroquois had told them about a waterway below Lake Erie that they called the Oyo, or "great river," that might lead them to the Far East. Although two centuries had passed since Christopher Columbus had first traveled west to try and find new trade routes to China, the lure of valuable spices, silks, and other riches still enticed many explorers. In 1669, a group of Frenchmen, led by René-Robert Cavelier, Sieur de La Salle, canoed down the St. Lawrence River hoping to find their way to the East. While they were not successful, the explorers found themselves in a wooded land rich with wild animals and exotic plant life. Soon afterward, the region north of the "Oyo" River and west of the Appalachians was christened "Ohio." Cavelier decided to continue exploring what would later be called the Mississippi River. Some of his companions, however, realized they could make their fortunes in this new territory. Ohio had a plentiful beaver population, and beaver fur was quite fashionable in Europe at the time. The French explorers, assisted by some Native Americans, trapped and skinned the animals, whose pelts were then sold to European fur traders.

According to Henry Howe, author of *Historical Collections of Ohio: An Encyclopedia of the State*, the French retained a hold on the region for many years but never bothered to establish any type of civil or criminal court system. Their interest apparently was not building permanent settlements; rather, they seemed focused on reaping whatever rewards the land had to offer. Before long, the British became aware of Ohio's rich potential and soon challenged France for control of the region. Battles first erupted there between the opposing forces in the late 1600s. But more than fifty years would pass before the most violent conflict, which became known as the French and Indian War (1754–63).

By the mid eighteenth century, the French resented the fact that the English were moving permanently into the region, cutting down trees and plowing the wilderness into farmland. They enlisted the willing aid of many Native American tribes, who were being forced out by the English settlers. But Great Britain, already aware that rebellion was brewing across America's coast, sent a large number of troops into the region, eventually forcing France to concede. The English hoped to retain ownership of at least part of the New World as their control of the thirteen American colonies weakened. For a time, British soldiers exerted military authority in Ohio over both the Native Americans and the European settlers, even though many disputes were settled and criminals were punished without their intervention. After losing the Revolutionary War (1775–83), England signed the Treaty of Paris, relinquishing all rights to the territory. Before long, the area, with its growing cities, rich farmland, and vast network of waterways, became a hub of American business and industry.

Unfortunately, crime continued to arrive in Ohio along with the constant stream of settlers who moved there in the eighteenth and nineteenth centuries. Even after it officially became a part of the United States in 1803, there were often too many people living too far from civilization for them to seek out justice in its newly established court system. Christened the "Buckeye State," primarily for the flowering tree commonly known as the Ohio Buckeye, the new state was plagued by outlaws who often terrorized the pioneers. While crimes such as assault and horse theft were documented in the region's newspapers, one of the more unusual cases to occur in Ohio was a report of witchcraft related by Howe in his book.

EXPLORING OHIO'S CRIMINAL HISTORY

During the eighteenth and early nineteenth century, criminals in the Buckeye State could expect to incur serious punishment if they were caught breaking the law. Whipping was common; the number of lashes depended on the type of crime that had been committed. A first offender could be whipped no more than thirty times, while fifty was considered the maximum amount for a second offense. Unfortunately, as more settlers moved to the state, officials soon realized that they needed a more permanent solution to the growing crime rate, so in 1815, Ohio opened its first state penitentiary. Like many states, it used a system of solitary confinement that was supposed to give inmates a chance to repent their crimes.

The first penitentiary was built on ten acres of ground on the south side of Columbus, the state capital. It featured a thirty-by-sixty-foot, three-story brick building with cells for the inmates located on the top floor, and a one-hundred-square-foot exercise yard that was surrounded by a stone wall about fifteen feet high. Three years later, the prison was doubled in

In 1814, a wealthy farmer who bred horses soon noticed that many of his animals suffered from distemper, a viral disease that affected their internal organs. When the Mill Creek resident was unable to cure any of his stock, he became convinced that they had been cursed by a witch. The farmer decided that the person who was casting spells on his horses was an elderly lady, Mrs. Garrison, who lived about ten miles from his farm. To counteract her magic, he was advised to shoot one of his horses with a silver bullet in order to cure the animal and kill the witch. According to Howe, "The mare, of course, was killed; and as it so happened, that, in a very short time after, poor Mrs. Garrison died, the experiment was declared to be successful, and the experimenter believes to this day that his silver bullet killed the poor old woman." Howe noted, however, that the old woman, who had already been in poor health, probably died from natural causes. The farmer was never charged with any crime.

size and workshops were added as a way to generate income. The inmates were employed in woodworking, weaving, gunsmithing, and other useful trades. It was also the home of Ohio's Death Row: Prisoners were executed by hanging at the penitentiary until 1897 when the electric chair came into use.

There were occasional escape attempts, but according to Henry Howe, author of *Historical Collections of Ohio in Two Volumes: An Encyclopedia of the State*, the most notable one occurred in 1830. Howe wrote, "One day, about a dozen prisoners, under the leadership of a daring fellow, Smith Maythe by name, secreted themselves near the outer door of the prison, and when the turnkey unlocked the door, Maythe sprang upon him, securing a firm hold, while his companions rushed out." Maythe followed the other inmates to a woods just south of the prison, but they were all soon captured.

Although many of Ohio's first jails and prisons have either decayed or been demolished, some preservation groups are hard at work restoring

(continued on page 6)

these buildings that reflect a unique aspect of the state's past. Some of the jails are simple wooden structures—familiar as those once seen on Saturday afternoon westerns—while others are examples of Victorian-era elegance that often housed the jailer along with the jailed.

One of the state's best-known facilities that has been preserved is Mansfield Reformatory, located about eighty miles southwest of Cleveland. The huge Gothic stone building was built by Levi T. Scofield in 1896. The architect hoped that the physical environment would help to inspire inmates to repent their crimes and embrace a more productive lifestyle. He apparently didn't succeed, because the prison's population continued to grow as more people moved to the Buckeye State. The reformatory was in operation for almost a century; the last inmates were moved in 1990 to the new Mansfield Correctional Institute, which was built right behind the

As in most states, Ohio's early law was often guided by religious principles. One common statute, still enforced in many regions today, was closing all businesses on Sunday and refraining from any activity on that day that was not related to church. As Lawrence M. Friedman noted in *Crime and Punishment in American History*, "Ohio law in 1831 did not allow anyone above the age of fourteen to engage in 'sporting, rioting, quarreling, hunting, fishing, shooting, or . . . at common labor' on Sunday, except for 'works of necessity and charity.' It was also an offense for a tavernkeeper to sell liquor on Sunday, except to travelers."

In 1833, Ohio's fledgling criminal justice system was tested by a member of a gang of horse thieves who were terrorizing southwestern Ohio. Area residents suspected that Walter G. Perry, who lived in Guernsey County, matched the description of a thief who had stolen a horse from William Knappenburger, a farmer from Tuscarawas County, on October 15 of that year. Knappenburger offered a reward to anyone who captured the suspect but Perry disappeared soon after warrants were issued for his arrest. The suspect eluded authorities for months, but on January 5, 1834, he was tracked to his reformatory. In addition to history and architecture buffs, the penitentiary attracts both amateur and professional paranormal investigators, who believe it is haunted by the ghosts of prisoners past. For further information, contact Mansfield Reformatory, 100 Reformatory Road, Mansfield, OH 44905, (419) 522-2644, or visit the website at www.mrps.org.

Another intriguing stop for anyone interested in the history of crime is the Cleveland Police Museum, operated by the Cleveland Police Historical Society in the Justice Center at 1300 Ontario Avenue in downtown Cleveland. Featuring exhibits about noted lawman Eliot Ness and notorious cases such as the Kingsbury Run murders, the museum is open Mondays through Fridays from 10 A.M. to 4 P.M. and offers guided tours. For further information, call (216) 623-5055 or e-mail clevelandpolicemus1@ roadrunner.com.

hideout in the woods outside of the McElroy district. Following his capture, a defiant Perry was tried and sentenced on April 19, 1834, in the courthouse in Tuscarawas County.

While horse thieves were often punished with hanging, Perry instead was initially sentenced to five years in prison. The prisoner had been wounded during his arrest, however, and when his leg refused to heal properly, the governor pardoned him after a year. After he returned home, the entire Perry clan reportedly disappeared from the region. Local residents learned afterward that Perry was more than just a horse thief; he had also been involved with counterfeiters who were operating in the region. At a time when many different types of coins from different countries were commonly used, it was easy for counterfeiters to produce their own and place them in circulation.

Settlers in Ohio's rural regions were not the only ones confronted by crime at that time. Mob violence, which was also occurring in other states, repeatedly erupted in one of Ohio's major cities. Despite laws against rioting, the offices of a three-month-old Cincinnati newspaper, the *Philanthropist*, were broken into in mid

July, 1836, and the printing press was destroyed. On July 30, a group gathered at the corner of Main and Seventh Streets and invaded the newspaper offices once again, tearing apart the press and destroying other property. According to Howe, "A portion of the press was dragged down Main street, broken up and thrown into the river." As that occurred, more office equipment was piled at the center of Main Street with plans for a bonfire, which was averted at the last minute. What had provoked these repeated attacks against the paper? The reason was the abolition of slavery, which was a highly controversial topic in the state in the years leading up to the Civil War. Apparently, the mob did not agree with the paper's anti-slavery stance. Once the offices were destroyed, the angry crowd went hunting for the editor, James G. Birney, and the printer, A. Pugh. Along the way, they tried to attack some African Americans who lived in Church Alley, but rapidly dispersed when they were greeted with gunfire.

In September 1841, another riot broke out in Cincinnati when fighting escalated between some Irish settlers and some African Americans. After a crowd of whites invaded a black neighborhood to try and find one of the men involved in the initial confrontation, the African American community mobilized and took to the streets. The mob was greeted with hostility and it wasn't long before gunfire erupted. Three days passed before local authorities were able to restore peace. They arrested about 250 members of the mob, forcing the rest to disperse. But as a precaution, the military was brought in to patrol the city in the days that followed.

Seven years later, Cincinnati was the scene of another riot, but this one did not erupt over race. Instead, it centered around two ex-soldiers who had returned to the city after serving in the Mexican War. The men had boarded with a family of German immigrants and were later charged with sexually assaulting their eleven-year-old daughter. Cincinnati residents were reportedly so outraged that they stormed the jail, ready to lynch both men for the heinous crime. Although ordered to withdraw, the crowd refused and fighting broke out. Eleven people died during the confrontation before the military was able to dispel the mob. The two men were ultimately released several months later when it was discovered that they had been falsely accused by the German immigrants. Apparently, the family had persuaded their daughter to lie to blackmail the men into signing over the 160 acres they had each received as payment for their time in the military. Before they could be charged, however, the family fled the city.

By the mid nineteenth century, Ohio's population had grown to more than one million. While new settlers still arrived almost daily in the Buckeye State, others had well-established roots in their communities by that time. But even then, the public faces some people presented were not the same as the ones they wore in private. In 1857, residents of the tiny town of Sylvania were shocked to learn they harbored a serial killer in their midst. Situated in Lucas County on the outskirts of the city of Toledo, Sylvania was founded around 1835 by General David White. In 1832, White was one of the first to move there and buy a large tract of land that would later become known as Sylvania, which is Latin for "woodlands." Predominantly settled by hardworking German, Irish, and English immigrants, the town quickly developed a thriving main street where many businesses were located. Peace in the tiny community was shattered in 1857, when Return Jonathan Meigs Ward was convicted of the gruesome murder of his wife, Olive. Ward, a tailor by trade, had been married twice before he and Olive wed. His first wife had died and his second wound up in an insane asylum.

Ward and Olive had only known each other for a few days before they wed, but she apparently thought he would be a good provider for her and her two children from a previous marriage. Unfortunately, the tailor soon proved to be an abusive spouse, who strongly disliked her eight-year-old son and three-year-old daughter. The couple quarreled constantly after settling into a tiny one-story house on Division Street. In November 1856, Olive left him and moved back to Adrian, Michigan, where she had previously lived, but according to Gaye E. Gindy, author of *Murder in Sylvania, Ohio*,

Ward apparently was not ready to let her go. After they had been separated for a few months, he persuaded Olive to come back to Sylvania, but he didn't know she had an ulterior motive when she agreed to return. Gindy noted, "Her plan was to go to Ward's house, get her clothes and other valuables and then go back to Adrian." Olive arrived in Sylvania on January 31, 1857. Soon afterward, she disappeared.

In the days that followed Olive's disappearance, Ward exhibited strange behavior that alarmed his neighbors so much that they alerted the sheriff. When inquiries were made about his wife, Ward declared that Olive had left town by train on February 3. That proved to be a lie and authorities soon uncovered other holes in his story. Two weeks later, the *Daily Toledo Blade* reported that after a thorough search of Ward's house, law enforcement had discovered "many bones" mixed in with the fireplace ashes that had been thrown out by the tailor. The paper noted, "It is now supposed that Ward not only murdered the woman, but that he had burned up the remains so far as he could." Before long, local papers were reporting in loving detail the sensational trial that followed. The case even spawned a "penny dreadful," as early tabloid magazines were known, titled *The Triple Murderer—The Life and Confessions of Return J. M. Ward.*

After his arrest, the tailor had in fact admitted that he had fatally struck his wife in the head with a flat-iron during an argument. Ward claimed he had acted in self-defense after his wife tried to hit him with a stick of hickory wood. He apparently never explained why he then dismembered her body and cremated her remains in the household stove. While the incident stunned Ward's neighbors, Sylvania residents were even more surprised to learn that Ward had confessed to committing two other murders after he was convicted of killing Olive. In 1851, while he worked in a tavern in Richland County, Ward said, he killed a merchant named Noah Hall to rob him of $800, which was a substantial amount of money at the time. Ward also admitted that, the following year, he had invited a peddler to spend the night at his house—an uncharacteristic gesture of generosity on his part. After the man retired, Ward struck him on the head with an axe and stole $50 from him. According to the June 12, 1857, issue of the *Daily Toledo Blade*, "He then took a dry goods box, which he had in the yard and packing the dead man in it put it under his bed in his own room and went to bed." Ward then threw the body into Lake Huron. While some would later wonder about his involvement in the first murder, no one ever suspected him of committing the second. Just before noon on June 12, 1857, Ward was hanged at the Lucas County Jail for killing his wife.

While the Ward case was talked about for months, not every murder received such ongoing public attention. On October 2, 1868, the *Cincinnati Commercial* briefly reported, "James Hoban, a Cleveland saloon-keeper, was stabbed, it is supposed fatally, on Tuesday, by Jas. English and John Wetmore. Hoban's wife, in attempting to help her husband, received dangerous cuts." Interestingly enough, it was common at that time for even out-of-state newspapers to carry such stories. On February 25, 1871, the *Kennebec Reporter* in Gardiner, Maine, reported, "Major Fisk of the Cliff House at Rocky river, Ohio, was shot and killed, Thursday evening by a German girl named Fanny Droz, who charges that Fisk seduced and abandoned her. She is now in custody."

Although the Civil War was over by this time, race was still a volatile subject for many people in Ohio. The *Baltimore Weekly Sun* reported this on July 23, 1871:

A colored man named Charles Hammond, of Darke county, on Saturday pursued Miss Clay, who was passing to a neighboring house, and ravished her. He has been arrested and lodged in jail. It has since been discovered he made improper advances to two girls near Union City, aged 13 and 15 respectively, while the latter were gathering blackberries, and overpowering the younger, was only prevented from carrying out his designs by her youth. Intense excitement prevails at Greenville, where he is a prisoner. It is generally believed the wretch will be lynched.

Such "frontier justice" was exercised on a regular basis in Ohio during the late nineteenth century, regardless of the criminal's race. The *Ohio Democrat* reported on August 1, 1873, that Jeff Davis, also known as John Miller, had been shot by the constable the preceding month. A notorious outlaw, Davis had apparently attempted to assault "Miss Hunierickhouse, who was in the company of another girl, on the public highway, in the vicinity of Ragersville." Davis was arrested by Constable D. Neff about six miles south of Newcomerstown "at the house of a widow woman." His body was later hung from a tree as a warning to other outlaws.

As settlers continued to move westward, the court system began to step in more often to administer justice. In 1898, Howe wrote, "At present there are ten Apache Indians sent here by the United States authorities to serve sentences of from ten to thirty years for manslaughter. We were informed that they had killed a number of their own race, members of a hostile tribe, in revenge for some injury done."

While life on the frontier may have remained harsh, city life in the late nineteenth century was not always tame. In *The Killer in the Attic*, John Stark Bellamy II noted that while many horrible crimes

IT'S ILLEGAL TO DO WHAT?

Every state in America has its share of outdated laws that are still on the books but, fortunately, rarely enforced. Here are some of the sillier state laws in Ohio:

- Women are prohibited from wearing patent leather shoes in public (to prevent men from looking up their skirts).
- It is illegal to get a fish drunk.
- Residents are prohibited from participating in or conducting a duel.
- No one may be arrested on Sunday or on the Fourth of July.

occurred in Cleveland in the 1800s, "For sheer cussedness, mayhem, and gore galore, there is nothing to beat William Adin's triple-murder bloodbath on December 4, 1875." Like Return Ward, Adin did not have a happy home life, a fact that he frequently shared with anyone who would listen. That day, the fifty-six-year-old businessman walked to the neighborhood fire station, where he complained about his domestic troubles to firefighter Otto Schuardt. According to Bellamy, Adin said that his wife Barbara was stealing from him and his twenty-three-year-old stepdaughter Hattie was encouraging her, causing frequent arguments between husband and wife. Their constant disputes had finally forced Hattie to move in with some friends. When his monologue was interrupted by the tolling of the fire station clock, Adin declared to Schuardt that it was time for him to go home—and settle things once and for all.

Returning to his house on the corner of Scranton and Starkweather shortly after six that morning, Adin quarreled with his wife over money. He claimed that she had taken funds he needed to pay their property taxes. When she refused to give him any money, Adin picked up a claw hammer and an axe that stood in a corner of the kitchen and furiously beat his wife to death. Hiding the body, he

Not to be outdone, individual cities have added some unique laws of their own: In Akron, it is illegal to display colored chickens for sale, and in Bay Village, it is against the law to walk a cow down Lake Road. If a Canton resident loses his pet tiger, he must notify authorities within one hour. In Cleveland, it's illegal to catch mice without a hunting license, while McDonald residents are not allowed to parade ducks down Ohio Avenue. Anyone who lives in North Canton is supposed to notify the police before they strap on their roller skates. In Oxford, it is illegal to drive around the town square more than one hundred times at once. Finally, while Toledo outlaws throwing snakes at people, Paulding police officers are authorized to bite any dog that refuses to stop barking.

stashed the hammer in his wagon and drove off to find his step-daughter, who was then living with Elizabeth and George Benton. Adin stalked into the Bentons' kitchen, where he demanded Hattie return home with him. When she refused, Adin pulled out the hammer and beat her to death. Elizabeth Benton attempted to intervene, and Adin turned on her as well.

When authorities later investigated the crime, they discovered that Adin's accusations against his family may have hidden a darker motive for his actions. It seemed that his wife Barbara was apparently so tired of his physical and mental abuse that she was on the verge of divorcing him, which meant Adin would have had to share the family's assets. And before she moved out, Hattie had accused him of making sexual advances toward her. The more she rejected him, the more obsessed he became. Adin, who never showed any signs of remorse, claimed that the three women had driven him to commit murder. He was later convicted on all three charges and hanged shortly after noon on June 22, 1876, at the Central Police Station on Franklin Street. His body was buried in an unmarked graved in Woodland Cemetery's potter's field.

Of course, not every crime was as tragic. It seemed that joyriding, a common occurrence after the arrival of the automobile, was a problem even in the 1800s. On April 16, 1877, the *Cleveland Leader* reported, "Michael Stacey and George Klein were arrested on Saturday morning for taking and wrongfully using Thomas Kirchmer's horse and wagon."

During this period, Ohio residents had a lot to be proud of. The state's first professional baseball team, the Cincinnati Redstockings, was founded in 1869, and The Ohio State University was given its charter the following year. And who could forget about Ohio native Thomas Edison, who invented the electric light bulb in 1879? Unfortunately, such positives didn't always outweigh the growing crime rate in the Buckeye State. Even in the late nineteenth century, the public was still quick to take the law into its hands if a criminal was not suitably punished by the courts. On March 28, 1884, a mob invaded the jail on Sycamore Street in Cincinnati, intending to lynch William Berner for the murder of his employer, William Kirk. The crowd was apparently furious because Berner had only been convicted of manslaughter, instead of murder. According to Howe, the lawyers who had defended Berner for this "dastardly, cold-blooded crime" were guilty of attempting to suborn testimony, bribing jury members, and other unethical acts. When Berner was convicted of the lesser charge, mass meetings were held throughout the city, condemning the verdict.

The mob arrived too late at the jail to administer justice because Berner had already been removed from the building. That didn't stop the angry residents from attacking the courthouse throughout the weekend, though. In the meantime, Berner had managed to escape from Deputy Sheriff Dominick Devots, who had been assigned as his escort, but he was captured a few days later in the woods outside of Loveland. When he was returned to prison, a mob broke into the courthouse once again and set fire to the building. The military was ordered into Cincinnati to restore peace, and Berner was removed to the state penitentiary at Columbus to begin serving his twenty-year sentence.

By the late 1800s, more laws were passed by the state legislature to enforce specific moral standards. In 1885, Ohio passed an obscenity law that made it a crime to distribute any publication that featured stories of crime or included police reports. In addition, further statutes were enacted to "protect" women from men who might want to take advantage of them. It hadn't been that long since pioneer women had tilled the earth, fought off Indian attacks, and survived all types of natural disasters while raising their families. But now they were stereotyped as being too frail to function on their own. In 1886, any male teacher who took advantage of his position to seduce a female student could face up to ten years in jail. Ironically, in the years that followed, this attitude would ultimately work to the advantage of women lawbreakers, who were usually given less harsh sentences than men. In 1844, Esther Foster had been the first woman executed for murder in the Buckeye State, but almost a century would pass before the death penalty was carried out against another woman.

By the turn of the twentieth century, the population of Ohio had grown to more than four million. The new century brought further growth and development within the state as well as pride over the re-election of William McKinley to his second term as the twenty-fifth President of the United States. Unfortunately, that pride was short-lived when McKinley was assassinated on September 6, 1901, by another Ohio resident. Leon Czolgosz was the son of Polish immigrants who owned a small farm in Ohio. After studying anarchist philosophies for about a year, he believed that the only way to call attention to the lives of the poor in America was by a dramatic gesture—shooting the president. While standing in line at the Pan American Exposition in Buffalo, New York, waiting to shake hands with the president, Czolgosz pulled out a pistol and shot McKinley twice. The president lingered for eight days before he died, but sadly, it was probably not the bullet wounds that killed him. He developed gangrene of the pancreas after not receiving needed medical treatment. Convicted on September 23 of first-degree murder, Czolgosz went defiantly to the electric chair in Auburn Prison in Auburn, New York, on October 29. His last words were "I am not sorry."

McKinley's assassination was shocking, but it was far from the last of such incidents to mar life in Ohio. In 1903, Cleveland-area residents were stunned by the killing of forty-year-old Agatha Reichlin, a devout Catholic who kept house for her two older brothers at a parsonage on the southwest corner of Reid and 8th Streets in Lorain. She was brutally beaten to death inside the rectory by an unknown assailant, shortly after retiring on the night of April 30. What scandalized the city was the fact that another priest, Rev. Ferdinand Walser, who was filling in for her brother, Rev. Charles W. Reichlin, may have been responsible for the horrible crime. At about that same time, the Mafia was spreading throughout Ohio, killing anyone who tried to stop them from gaining control over both legitimate and illegitimate businesses. The advent of Prohibition gave the mob the opportunity to make a fortune through the sale of alcohol. But for some, neither the Roaring Twenties nor the Great Depression that followed had as much impact as the story of Anna Marie Hahn. She was a beautiful German immigrant who was determined to acquire the better things in life, even if she had to kill to get them.

CHAPTER 2

The Blonde Borgia

She was young, pretty, and on her way to America, free at last of family constraints. But little did Anna Marie Hahn expect she would become the most notorious woman in Ohio just because she discovered a talent for parting older men from their money—and their lives.

When Anna Marie Filser boarded the SS *Munchen* in Germany in February 1929, she left behind her parents, a sister, two brothers, and her three-year-old son Oscar, the result of a brief affair that she claimed had been with a married Viennese doctor. Born on July 7, 1906, Anna was blonde, attractive, and just a little spoiled by her family. She never understood why they were embarrassed by her decision to keep her illegitimate child. The Filsers, who were always concerned about their social status in the small community of Feussen, breathed a collective sigh of relief when she left. They hoped that their wayward youngest child would settle down once she moved in with relatives in Ohio. But Anna apparently had plans of her own, and they didn't involve a dull domestic life. America may have been spiraling into the Great Depression, but she was going to do more than just survive.

After her arrival, the twenty-two-year-old newcomer immediately caught the train from New York to Cincinnati. Anna was enthralled by the city, which was so different from her hometown. Founded in 1788 on the north shore of the Ohio River, Cincinnati had become a Midwestern center of industry and culture with a population that had grown to almost half a million people. Moving into the German District with her Aunt Anna and Uncle Max Doeschel, Anna was advised that she should find work as a housekeeper as soon as possible. After all, the Doeschels had sent $236 for her boat fare, a small fortune in those days, and they expected to be repaid.

For about a month, Anna stayed with the Doeschels in the house at 3540 Evanston Avenue that they shared with her cousins Ida and Richard Pfeffer. Then, according to Diana Britt Franklin, author of *The Good-bye Door*, "without a word to anyone Anna Marie suddenly moved out—'ran away,' she admitted—securing a furnished room on Walnut Street between Central Parkway and Twelfth Street." Anna rarely saw her relatives after that, and the Doeschels eventually realized she had no intention of paying back the money they had loaned her. Happy to be free of her relatives, the young immigrant soon had a long line of admirers who were ready to help her whenever she needed a few dollars for rent—or for the racetrack. Anna, it seemed, had quickly developed a gambling habit after her arrival in America. She became a frequent visitor to Ohio casinos; her favorite sporting event was horse racing. She dreamed that a big win at the track would soon allow her to bring her young son to America.

In 1929, Anna worked for a few weeks as a chambermaid at the Hotel Alms, but she continued to live well beyond her means thanks to the "loans" she still received from friends. One in particular was willing to open not just his wallet but also his home. She soon quit her job and moved into a room in an apartment at 304 East Fourteenth Street that belonged to Charles "Karl" Osswald. Anna told her friends that she was going to take care of "Uncle Charlie," as she called the seventy-one-year-old retired baker, who had lost his wife on April 3 of that year. Osswald was delighted to have such a pretty woman, who claimed to have nursing experience, looking after him. Anna kept house and provided the widower with good cooking and flirtatious company that for him quickly turned to love. She agreed to marry him that November, but she would first need one token of his affection: Anna asked Osswald to transfer his ninety-nine shares of Union Gas and Electric stock into her name. He readily agreed and also was happy to give her money whenever she asked. Before long, she was risking up to $50 a day of her benefactor's savings at the track—an amount that took many people in those days a week to earn.

With money in her pocket and plenty of time on her hands, Anna loved to stroll past the many sights of Cincinnati or frolic at the nearby Coney Island amusement park, usually with a male companion in tow. Shortly after moving in with Osswald, she met twenty-six-year-old Philip Hahn at a dance. The short, slender telegraph operator who worked for Western Union had a quiet, unassuming manner and couldn't believe he could win the heart of such a beautiful woman. Anna told her friends that Hahn was the type of man she wanted to settle down with, someone she knew would be a good father to her son. More than likely, she saw Hahn as someone who would be easily dominated by a strong-willed woman. They married on May 5, 1930, in Buffalo, New York. She never told anyone, certainly not Osswald, that she planned to finance her new life with the $13,000 the retired baker had left her in his will. To Anna, the money was as good as hers since she already drew on it whenever she wanted to place a bet.

The following year, Anna used more of Osswald's money to return to Germany and collect her five-year-old son from her concerned family, who were apparently not happy with the reports they had been receiving about her from the United States. When Anna and Oscar arrived back in Cincinnati, they moved with Philip Hahn into a small house at 6332 Savannah Avenue in the College Hill district of the city. Since Hahn worked nights, Anna was free to do as she pleased during the day, bringing her son along as she finagled money from her friends or stopped to place a bet on an upcoming horse race. Surprisingly, more than a year passed before Osswald learned of Anna's marriage and the presence of her son. When he found out, he tried to take her to court, according to Franklin: "His suit, filed July 30, 1931, charged her with breach of promise and sought the return of the stock and cash, plus 6 percent interest." Anna apparently managed to charm Osswald into dropping the case, which was dismissed on February 21, 1934. After Osswald died at age seventy-seven on August 14, 1935, from Bright's disease and arteriosclerosis, Anna received a check of $1,000 as beneficiary of his insurance policy from the National Biscuit Company, where he had worked for many years. It was all that was left of his stocks and savings because everything else had already been appropriated by Anna.

Hahn grew tired of working for the telegraph company, so Anna sold most of the stocks she had obtained from Osswald and used the money to purchase a delicatessen at 3201 Colerain Avenue. Neither husband nor wife, however, had a head for business. She spent whatever meager profits they made on the horses, and the delicatessen soon closed its doors. Undeterred, the couple opened another delicatessen a few doors down at 3007 Colerain Avenue, but the new business didn't fare any better than the first. Part of the reason may have been that while the Hahns' marriage appeared happy on the surface, the young couple fought frequently over money. Her husband never seemed to understand that while Anna wanted money, she just didn't want to have to work for it. When some of their creditors began clamoring for repayment, she soon found an easy, if illegal, way to get rich quick.

In early 1935, a suspicious fire broke out at the delicatessen at 3007 Colerain Avenue. Although it didn't cause much damage, Anna still received $300 from the insurance company. Then, the

Hahn residence erupted into flames not once, but twice. According to Franklin, the first fire occurred on June 2, 1935, and the second on May 20, 1936. The insurance company paid Anna a little more than $2,000 for both incidents. It seemed that her home wasn't the only thing Anna was prepared to sacrifice to make some easy money. Hahn protested strongly when his beautiful wife tried to acquire a $25,000 life insurance policy on him, naming her as beneficiary. He already suspected that Anna was prepared to do almost anything to get what she wanted. As time passed, he grew increasingly afraid of her. It seemed he had good reason. Not long after he refused to cooperate, Hahn became seriously ill. Vomiting, with a high fever, and racked with constant pain, he asked his mother to take him to a hospital even though Anna declared she would nurse him at home. Hahn recovered after a few days in the hospital but began to keep his distance from his wife once he was discharged. Apparently realizing she had raised his suspicions, Anna decided it was time to find another target. She began looking for work as a housekeeper.

In 1932, she was employed by Ernst Kohler, a retired teamster who lived alone in a large brick house at 2590 Colerain Avenue in Cincinnati's Camp Washington district. The house was so big that Kohler lived on the third floor and rented out portions of the rest to different tenants. Despite his fears, Hahn moved there with his wife and her son into two rented rooms. While Anna kept house, her husband drove a taxi at night; so once again he had little idea of how she spent her days. He wasn't alone. What Kohler didn't realize was that the pretty young woman he had hired was more concerned with his savings than she was with keeping up with his laundry. But like others before him, Kohler was quickly charmed by Anna, and after knowing her for only a few weeks, he provided generously for her in his will.

When Kohler died on May 6, 1933, Anna inherited his house and all of its furnishings, as well as his savings account, valued at more than $13,000. Although his relatives were outraged, there was nothing they could do to oust the Hahns from the premises. What no one knew at the time was that Kohler had a little help moving from this world to the next. One of the tenants, Dr. Arthur Vos, never locked the door of his first-floor office at the end of the day, a mistake that soon proved fatal for his landlord. Anna helped herself to blank prescription pads and soon was forging the doctor's name to obtain a variety of drugs from different pharmacies in town. While no one suspected her at the time, it was later discovered that Kohler apparently received massive doses of morphine administered by his new housekeeper. Once Anna's first conquest was safely out of the way, she soon found other unsuspecting victims.

In the weeks that followed Kohler's death, Anna happily scammed friends and neighbors—sometimes out of their life savings. Before long, she began passing herself off once again as a visiting nurse for elderly patients. The next to fall prey to her charms was seventy-two-year-old Albert Palmer, who lived at 2416 Central Parkway. The retired railroad watchman first met Anna in 1936 at a local casino, where they both enjoyed gambling and betting on horse races. Soon, Palmer accompanied her and Oscar on day trips around the city, often ending with a meal at her house. Anna became his caretaker and soon managed to wangle large sums of money from her unsuspecting employer. She called them "loans," but as always, she had no intention of repaying them. At the same time, some of her other creditors had finally grown tired of waiting and were now clamoring that she return the money she had previously borrowed. When Palmer eventually joined their chorus, he fell violently ill after eating suppers that were prepared by his nurse. The former watchman developed diarrhea and stomach cramps that were so bad, he died on March 26, 1937. No record was found among his papers of the loans he had made to Anna.

Jacob Wagner, a seventy-two-year-old retired gardener, was initially skeptical after Anna turned up at his apartment at 1805 Race Street in the middle of May 1937. The smiling blonde claimed to be his niece who had news of other relatives from Germany, but Wagner was not interested. Anna was not dissuaded, however, and soon insinuated herself into his daily life. Wagner was quick to question her when bank books and other valuables started to disappear from his home. According to Franklin, "The passbooks were Anna Marie's variation of the bait-and-switch con game. She planned to take Wagner's passbook with $4,831 in it and give him in return, as security, her bankbooks showing a total of more than $15,000 on deposit. Actually, she had no money in the accounts at all."

When Wagner continued to ask questions, Anna helped him search the apartment and soon "found" the allegedly lost account book. Like her previous employer, Wagner was smitten by the young woman and was willing to forgive and forget. But on June 1, less than two weeks after they met, a neighbor saw Anna pouring a large glass of orange juice for Wagner one hot afternoon. That same night, Anna found him writhing in agony on his bed. Although he was vomiting and passing blood, she waited several hours before calling for a doctor. The retired gardener died two days later. Even though his beautiful "niece" hadn't been caring for him for that long, Anna was his sole beneficiary and received $17,000 in his will.

The self-appointed angel of mercy did not realize, however, that the residents of Cincinnati's close-knit German community were growing increasingly suspicious of her activities. Although the coroner's report initially listed heart disease as Wagner's cause of death, a friend of the deceased persuaded authorities to exhume the retired gardener's body and autopsy his remains. After visiting Wagner's neighborhood, the police learned that Anna had first approached Wagner claiming to be a long-lost niece. Some of Wagner's friends told the investigators that they were concerned about Anna's behavior because she had spent several hours alone in Wagner's apartment after his death.

During the course of the investigation, the police met Olive Luella Koehler, an older woman who lived in Wagner's apartment building. Unlike the other residents, she was a staunch supporter of Anna's because the younger woman had been kind to her. On two occasions, Anna had bought her ice cream cones. But authorities were alarmed when Koehler related that she had become violently ill after eating the second cone—so bad, in fact, that she had to be admitted to the hospital. During Koehler's hospital stay, someone had stolen a bag from her apartment that contained jewelry and cash, but she doubted that her new friend had anything to do with the theft. Shortly afterward, another Cincinnati resident who was unable to resist Anna was sixty-seven-year-old George Gsellman, who bequeathed her $15,000 after he died on July 6, 1937, in his room at 1717 Elm Street. No one, however, could produce any real evidence that Anna had been involved in any wrongdoing related to his death.

Where was Anna's husband while she was busy keeping house for different men? He had returned to working nights for Western Union as a messenger and file clerk, earning about $10 a week. While Hahn's new job allowed him to avoid his wife, it is very possible that he was suspicious of her activities. Authorities later learned that Hahn probably kept silent in order to save his own life. Anna's subsequent suitor was not so fortunate.

George Obendoerfer was the next man to mistakenly believe that he had won Anna's heart. He was delighted when she invited him to travel out west with her and her son to find a new home that he could share with them. But by the time they arrived in Colorado Springs, the retired cobbler was so ill that he could not even walk without assistance. As he writhed in pain in his room at the Park Hotel, Anna and Oscar enjoyed the local sights—at his expense. When the money was gone, she abandoned him in a Colorado hospital, professing to authorities that she had never before met the man. Authorities questioned Anna after Obendoerfer died and their suspicions were aroused by her behavior and a story that kept changing almost daily. The police quickly ordered an autopsy that revealed high levels of arsenic in Obendoerfer's body. Apparently, the elderly man, along with two unknown companions, had checked into the Park Hotel on July 30, 1937. Colorado authorities strongly suspected that his arrival in the city was connected to the fact that the owner of the hotel had just filed a report claiming someone had stolen two diamond rings valued at $300.

Police soon learned that Obendorfer's companions at the Park Hotel were a woman named Anna Marie Hahn and her son. According to the hotel owner, Anna had said she lived in Cincinnati and was in Colorado on vacation. But when the authorities tried to locate her, they were surprised to find she and Oscar had disappeared. In the meantime, the police were alerted that a woman and a boy, matching the Hahns' description, had been visiting local pawn shops, trying to sell two diamond rings. They also discovered that Anna had unsuccessfully tried to withdraw $1,000 of her "husband's" money from a Denver bank, using a Cincinnati bankbook in the name of George Obendorfer.

Authorities in Colorado soon issued a warrant for Anna for suspicion of grand larceny in the theft of the hotel jewelry. They alerted the police in Cincinnati, who picked up Anna as soon as she returned to the city. When asked by investigators what she knew about George Obendorfer's death, Anna at first claimed not to know him. When they advised her that she had signed him in to the same hotel where she had stayed, Anna admitted that she met him on the train from Denver. She said she felt sorry for him because he was alone and obviously not in good health. The police knew Obendorfer was from Cincinnati, however, and learned from his relatives that he had been in good health until recently—when he began to date Anna Marie Hahn.

Obendorfer's relatives told police that he had traveled to Colorado with Anna, believing that they were going to a ranch she owned in Colorado Springs. When the investigators confronted her with this evidence, Anna admitted that she had in fact known Obendorfer, but that they were nothing more than casual friends. She declared once more that she had simply met him on the train and that it was pure coincidence that they were traveling to the same place. Anna said that Obendorfer became ill shortly after they arrived in Colorado and went to the hospital. After that, she had no further contact with him.

Unfortunately for Anna, her story of "accidentally" meeting Obendorfer on the train to Colorado unraveled after authorities questioned her son Oscar. The boy told police that his mother had in fact bought Obendorfer's ticket at Union Terminal in Cincinnati and that she had served the man several drinks while they were on the train. According to Oscar, Obendorfer got sick long before they arrived in Colorado.

When poison was discovered in Obendorfer's body, authorities exhumed both Wagner and Gsellman and found they had suffered the same fate. Gsellman's friends had told authorities he had become ill after Anna's last visit and died shortly thereafter. The coroner initially believed that the metallic poison discovered in the man's remains was arsenic. But further testing proved it was croton oil, one of the many home remedies that were popular around the turn of the twentieth century. Although a small dose was simply unpleasant, a large amount of the drug would be fatal. Croton oil caused, among other symptoms, an extreme burning sensation in the mouth, throat, and abdomen, as well as vomiting and bloody diarrhea before death. In Wagner's case, though, the autopsy revealed that he had ingested large quantities of arsenic.

As police continued their probe, the newspapers began publishing stories saying that Anna was the primary suspect in the deaths. They dubbed her the "Blonde Borgia," after the infamous Lucretia Borgia, who poisoned her enemies in Italy during the Renaissance. From prison, Anna happily gave interviews and posed for photographs, sometimes with her son by her side. The other inmates and even some of the staff treated her like royalty and Anna seemed to thrive on the attention. Stories ran in newspapers throughout the country, detailing Anna's life behind bars and the status of the investigation.

After reading the newspaper accounts, sixty-two-year-old George Heis stepped forward and told authorities that he had met

Anna the preceding year and had become violently ill after she
served him a mug of beer. A coal dealer for the Consolidated Coal
Company, Heis lived at 2922 Colerain Avenue, just a block away
from Anna. Like so many other men, Heis was immediately smitten
with the pretty blonde and only too happy to believe her when she
said she had divorced her husband. He loaned her more than $2,000
of his company's money over time, but his health began to fail when
he tried to collect on the debt. In the fall of 1936, still suffering a
variety of symptoms that he now suspected were the results of poison, Heis told Anna to stay away from his house. By the time Anna
went on trial, Heis had become a cripple confined to a wheelchair,
but he was glad to testify against the woman he had once adored.

In the meantime, the police continued to gather more evidence
against Anna. They canvassed the city and periodically searched the
Hahns' home. Their suspicions were confirmed when her husband
reluctantly turned over a half-ounce bottle of croton oil he had previously taken away from his wife. Suspecting that Anna had tried
to poison him, Hahn had kept the bottle hidden in a locker at work
for more than a year while he learned more about the drug. Authorities later discovered that Anna had purchased the oil on July 20,
1936, from a drug store in North College Hill. The pharmacist there
told police that Anna claimed her husband was a German druggist
who used the oil in his practice.

With Anna still safely in custody, Cincinnati police continued to
build their case against her for the deaths of the four local men. During a search of her home, they found the long-missing I.O.U. for
$2,000 that she had signed for money borrowed from Albert Palmer.
Authorities learned from Palmer's family that he had been sick for
quite a while before he died and that $4,000 was discovered to be
missing from his estate. They suspected that Anna, his attentive
nurse, had helped herself to the money.

To prevent Anna from being extradited to Colorado, Ohio
authorities arraigned her on August 10, 1937, and charged her with
the murder of Jacob Wagner. Dudley Outcalt, Loyal Martin, and

Simon Leis of the Hamilton County Prosecutor's Office would present the case in court against Anna, while she would be defended by Joseph H. Hoodin and Hiram Bosinger Sr. The trial began on October 11, 1937, before Common Pleas Court judge Charles S. Bell. According to Franklin, when Anna's twelve-year-old son and husband arrived in court, Hahn told her, "Regardless of our marital difficulties in the last few years, I absolutely believe in your innocence and will stick by you." Interestingly, the jury was composed of eleven women and just one man, an unusual occurrence for the time—and one that likely affected the ultimate outcome of the case.

In his opening remarks, Outcalt immediately declared that Anna had killed Jacob Wagner to obtain control of his money and estate. In the days that followed, witnesses took the stand and recounted Wagner's last agonizing days. According to www.trutv.com, the *Cincinnati Inquirer* stated a chemist testified that the victim had enough arsenic in him to kill four men. A handwriting expert told the court that Wagner's alleged "will" was actually a forgery composed in Anna's handwriting. Although she was being tried on just one count of murder, the judge allowed the prosecutors to introduce evidence that was related to the other poisoning cases to prove a pattern of homicidal behavior. George Heis was that last witness called to testify about his encounters with Anna before the prosecution rested on October 29.

Confronted by a mountain of evidence, the defense opened its case on Monday, November 1, 1937, by placing Anna on the stand. For three days, she told her version of her relationship with Wagner and refused to be swayed even during cross-examination. According to Franklin, "The defendant, dressed nun-like in a navy serge suit" was very composed for the entire time she was on the stand. When her attorney asked her about her relationship with Wagner, Anna said that he was a casual acquaintance who had occasionally performed yard work for her. She told the court that she had initially sought him out because she had received a letter for him from Germany, which had mistakenly been sent to her address. The defendant denied asking Wagner's neighbor, Elizabeth Colby, "Are there any old men here?" when she first arrived at his apartment building. She also swore that she had never added poison to anything the old man had eaten or drank.

With her hair neatly curled and her fingernails polished, courtesy of her fellow inmates, the accused appeared to be the picture of innocence. While the prosecution had taken more than two weeks to present its evidence, the defense rested its case on November 4.

During closing arguments, Outcalt painted Anna as a scheming, greedy, heartless woman who purposefully poisoned her victims to gain control of their money and property. Hoodin tried to refute the prosecutor's argument by telling the jury that the witnesses who had testified were already prejudiced against Anna before they took the stand; as a result, their words were tainted. His efforts to sway the jury proved unsuccessful. The panel returned in two hours with a unanimous vote of "guilty with no recommendation of mercy." That meant Anna would automatically face the death penalty for the murder of Jacob Wagner. Motionless as the verdict was read, Anna was then returned to her jail cell.

Anna appeared before Judge Bell the following week and once again declared her innocence when she was given the opportunity to address to court. While he was obviously uncomfortable at the thought of sentencing a woman to death, the judge pronounced that on March 10, 1938, she would die in the electric chair at the Ohio State Penitentiary in Columbus. Transferred to the prison on December 1, 1937, Anna—as the only woman inmate on Death Row—was provided with the following creature comforts, according to Franklin: "There was a white cast-iron bed, a rocking chair, a large table where she could eat her meals and write her letters, a second chair . . . and next to the bed a small table on which someone had placed a Bible." In addition, she was given a private bathroom where she could only be observed by the matron on duty.

Anna's attorneys filed so many appeals on her behalf that her sentence was not carried out on the initial date. On December 7, the

Evening Gazette of Xenia reported that her counsel was arguing that afternoon for a writ of habeas corpus at the courthouse in Columbus before federal judge Mell G. Underwood. According to the paper, "The habeas corpus action, filed by Attorneys Joseph Hoodin, Sidney Kahn and Sidney Brant, contended that Mrs. Hahn's constitutional rights were denied when the prosecution in her trial introduced evidence on four murders instead of one." But judges in both the Ohio courts and later the United States Supreme Court refused to block the execution of Prisoner No. 73228, which had already been rescheduled for 8 P.M. that same night. An appeal to Ohio governor Martin L. Davey also met with no success. A copy of the governor's statement was printed in the newspaper and quoted him as saying, "I was brought up to respect womanhood and cannot escape the feeling that there is a little difference when a woman is involved in a tragedy of this kind." At the same time, Davey declined to intervene on Anna's behalf, even thought he internally "rebelled" at the idea of sentencing a woman to death.

As she awaited word from her attorneys, Anna sat neatly dressed, with her nails polished and her hair styled, greeting reporters and prison personnel who came to her cell like a benevolent queen. Like most people, she believed that she would never actually be executed for her crimes simply because she was a woman. But in the hours beforehand, she wrote four letters that she entrusted to her lawyers. Although she had displayed little emotion during the trial, the notorious Blonde Borgia fell apart when it came time to take that final walk to the electric chair. Entering the chamber on shaky legs, Anna passed out and collapsed to the floor. After she was awakened with an ammonia capsule and strapped into the chair, Anna cried and begged for release.

She had professed her innocence to the end of her trial, but the letters included a confession of her crimes. Two weeks after Anna's execution, Hoodin announced that the letters she had given him on the night of her execution had been sold to the *Cincinnati Enquirer* and the money had been put into a trust to support her young son.

The next day, the paper announced that they would be publishing the letters on the following two days. In one, Anna admitted her responsibility for the death of the men who had been her benefactors:

> I don't know how I could have done the things I did in my life. Only God knows what came over me when I gave Albert Palmer that first one, the poison that caused his death. When I think of that poison even now, I feel a strange something come over me, something happens to my mind. . . . I do not try to excuse myself for my actions. They were not me at all. I have made my peace with God, and someday He will explain to me what caused my mind to become so warped to do these things. It all seems like a terrible dream.

In another, she blamed her actions on her concern for her son's welfare: "My husband and I had been out of work and I started worrying about my boy's future. I became crazy with fears that my boy and I would starve." But after borrowing large sums from Albert Palmer, Anna decided to repay him by giving him "a little of this" so that he would stop harassing her for the money. She noted: "I don't know what made me do it, but I slipped some of the poison in the oysters." Although she claimed to struggle with her actions, Anna went on to describe the way she had poisoned Jacob Wagner and her other victims. She closed the final letter: "I feel that God has shown me my wrongs in life and my only regret is that I have not the power to undo the trouble and heartache that I have caused." But like many other criminals, did Anna truly regret her actions or simply the fact that she had been caught?

Anna's son Oscar was eventually placed with a foster family in the Midwest and the money raised from the sale of his mother's letters was used for his support. The *Cincinnati Enquirer* apparently never revealed his new name or his whereabouts to the public. Although Phillip Hahn had stood by his wife during the trial, his voice was strangely silent when Oscar tried to appeal his mother's conviction. Not long after her execution, he was spotted around

Cincinnati accompanied by another woman. Anna's body was buried on December 8, 1938, in unsanctified ground at the Holy Cross Catholic Cemetery in Columbus. Her grave was later marked by a plain gray headstone made by inmates at the Ohio State Penitentiary.

A new breed of bank robber was born in the 1930s—one who often commanded the respect and assistance of the public, who saw the robbers as Robin Hoods attacking the corrupt upper classes. Two of the best known, John Dillinger and "Pretty Boy" Floyd, robbed banks in Ohio during the Great Depression. Born in Indianapolis, Indiana, on June 22, 1903, Dillinger was in prison by age twenty-two, where he became friends with veteran bank robbers like Harry Pierpont. Paroled in 1933, he immediately rounded up some friends and robbed the New Carlisle National Bank in New Carlisle of $10,000, a considerable fortune in those days. Later arrested at the Dayton home of his girlfriend, a divorcee named Mary Longnaker, Dillinger was sprung from the Allen County jail in Lima by his friends, who shot and killed the sheriff during the escape. A fugitive who managed to elude the law for almost a year after that, the infamous bank robber was fatally wounded by FBI agent Melvin Purvis as he left a movie theater in Chicago on July 22, 1934.

Charles Arthur "Pretty Boy" Floyd was born in Adairsville, Georgia, on February 3, 1904, but moved at a young age with his family to Oklahoma. He soon discovered that he preferred stealing to farming and by age twenty was part of a gang who robbed local merchants. In 1930, they descended on Ohio and held up the Farmers & Merchants Bank in Sylvania, escaping with about $2,000. Floyd and his cohorts continued to rob banks and businesses throughout northern Ohio until they were arrested in Akron. Later sentenced to fifteen years in prison, Floyd managed to escape from custody and soon formed another gang. He headed to Toledo but after a run-in with police, he left the state, vowing to never return.

Following the death of John Dillinger, Floyd decided it was time to leave the United States for good, but on October 20, 1934, as he and his companions were on their way to Mexico, they were forced by heavy fog to stop in Wellsville, a tiny town on the border of Pennsylvania. Alert local residents became suspicious of the well-dressed strangers and notified the sheriff, who in turn contacted the FBI. When Melvin Purvis arrived on the scene, he quickly organized a manhunt that ended two days later with the fatal shooting of Floyd outside of a farmhouse in East Liverpool. Although it made front page news, for many Ohio residents Floyd's death would pale in comparison to the horrors that would soon surface in the city of Cleveland.

CHAPTER 3

The Torso Murderer

Serial killers have haunted human society for generations. While some of them are caught, more than a few have slipped back into the shadows, their identities unknown even to this day. In the 1930s, one such phantom prowled the streets of Cleveland, terrorizing the city and frustrating one of America's top law enforcement officers.

Thousands of Americans lost everything when the Great Depression devastated the country. Homeless children wandered city streets, begging or stealing whatever they could to stay alive. Men and women moved wearily from state to state in search of work, hoping that their next stop would be the last. These "hobos," as they were commonly called, often camped on the outskirts of towns in makeshift shelters, providing each other with some sense of community while they waited for better days. On the east side of Cleveland, they gathered in an ancient ravine known as Kingsbury Run, situated about sixty feet below street level. Named for Jasper Kingsbury, who had settled in the area in 1797, it was a popular retreat filled with peaceful lakes in the nineteenth century but later became the site of a railroad route and many industries, including a crude oil refinery. By the 1930s, it was overflowing with weeds, trash, and transients who huddled around campfires beside homemade shacks.

At that time, Cleveland was the seventh largest city in America, with a population of more than one million people. Although most residents avoided Kingsbury Run as much as possible, two adventurous boys decided it was warm enough on September 23, 1935, to venture down to an embankment there that was known locally as Jackass Hill. According to Steven Nickel, author of *Torso: The Story of Eliot Ness and the Search for a Psychopathic Killer*, "shortly before five o'clock that bright afternoon, a pair of youths fresh from school—sixteen-year-old James Wagner and twelve-year-old Peter Kostura—were scampering along the southern cliffs of the Run." When they scrambled down the hill, Wagner noticed a patch of white in the grass and shouted for his friend. They found a naked, headless corpse half buried in the weeds, and immediately ran for help. According to www.trutv.com, "Detectives Emil Musil and Orly May were the first Cleveland policemen on the scene. They found not only one headless man, but two, both washed and drained of blood." The officers noted that the bodies were discovered at the foot of East 49th Street and Praha Avenue, and after an extensive search, their heads were discovered buried nearby. The penis had been cut off of each body and placed near one of the heads.

In addition, the police discovered bloodstained clothing, a torch, and a small metal bucket filled with oil at the scene. One of the bodies had been badly burned and was in an advanced state of decomposition. Coroner Arthur J. Pearse later noted that the victim, who had been dead for at least a week, had dark brown hair, was about 5 feet, 6 inches tall, and weighed about 165 pounds. He had still been alive when he was decapitated. The coroner stated that the second man was in his twenties with brown hair, blue eyes, and a light complexion. Standing about 5 feet, 11 inches, the second victim had weighed about 150 pounds, but unlike his companion, he had only been dead for two or three days. Rope burns on his wrists indicated that he had been tied up by his killer.

Authorities were unable to fingerprint the first man because of the condition of the body. Fingerprints lifted from the second victim identified him as twenty-eight-year-old Edward A. Andrassy, who, unlike most Kingsbury Run residents, had family ties to Cleveland. The son of Hungarian immigrants, Andrassy had once lived at 1744 Fulton Road. In 1928, he married a nurse he met at Cleveland City Hospital, where he had worked as an orderly in the psychiatric ward. After just a few years, he left his wife and quit his job at the hospital. Andrassy sold magazines for a while but was reportedly unemployed at the time he was murdered.

Joseph Andrassy, the victim's father, told police that the whole family had become concerned by Andrassy's recent abrupt change in lifestyle. After he stopped working, Andrassy moved home with his parents but often frequented the area of East Ninth Street and Bolivar Road, a known criminal hangout. Not long afterward, the father said Andrassy was arrested for carrying a concealed weapon and was also jailed several times for being drunk and disorderly. As the murder investigation continued, the police learned that the young man might have been either bisexual or homosexual. A number of witnesses came forward and claimed that he had male lovers, which was not socially acceptable at the time. Helen Andrassy, the victim's mother, said that threats had been made against her son's life by Italian mobsters just before he left home on Thursday, September 19, 1935, the last time Andrassy's parents saw him alive. The coroner believed the young man was probably killed the following day. Authorities were never able to identify the other victim, who was simply known afterward as "John Doe I" or "Victim One."

The police determined that both murders were probably crimes of passion and that the victims had probably been killed at another location before being taken to Kingsbury Run. They also believed that the two victims knew each other and were killed by the same person. The murderer would have had to be fairly strong; it was impossible to drive a car close to Jackass Hill, so he would have been forced to carry the bodies down the steep embankment. Some detectives speculated that a team of killers was involved, but that theory soon fell by the wayside. At the time, no one connected the two murders with another that had occurred the previous year. That was when part of a woman's torso, which had been in the water for about three months, appeared on the shore of Lake Erie near Euclid Beach. Dubbed "The Lady of the Lake" by the press, the woman was never officially considered to be a victim of the Kingsbury Run killer, although many officers later believed otherwise. Like the first male victim, her remains were never identified.

Unfortunately, even armed with information about Andrassy, the police were unable to uncover any further evidence that pointed to the identity of the murderer. The press dubbed the unknown suspect "The Mad Butcher," "The Torso Murderer," "The Headhunter," and "The Kingsbury Run Killer" and demanded to know when the streets of Cleveland would once again be safe. Although the police began pulling in suspects, they were always released, because no supporting evidence could be gathered against them. With little progress in the investigation, the story was soon pushed off the front pages of local newspapers. Public attention was caught by the mayoral election, which promised to bring change to Cleveland, a city plagued for many years by graft and corruption from city hall through individual neighborhoods. Police officers apparently looked the other way while the Mafia fought rival gangs for control of loan-sharking, narcotics, and other illegal activities, while theft, assault, and murder occurred routinely throughout the city.

The race for mayor was won by Harold Burton, a Republican who promised to oust crime from city hall and the police force, as well as the city's streets. To follow through on that promise, Mayor Burton appointed thirty-two-year-old Eliot Ness as his director of public safety shortly after he took office. Although some expressed doubt about the mayor's decision, Ness, with his hand-picked squad known as "The Untouchables," was already famous as the man who had successfully battled Al Capone and his bootleggers in Chicago during Prohibition. Burton believed that Ness's reputation as an incorruptible crime fighter would build trust in the city's government. The federal agent, born on April 19, 1903, in Chicago, had graduated from the University of Chicago in 1927 with dual degrees in business and law and later earned a master's degree in criminology from the university. He represented a new breed of law enforcement officer—educated and well-trained. But by the following month, the Torso Killer surfaced once again, almost as though in defiance of the mayor's plans.

On the bitter cold morning of January 26, 1936, the police received a call from Charles Paige, a butcher who owned the White Front Meat Market on Central Avenue. Paige reported that pieces of a body had been found in a bushel basket, wrapped in burlap, outside of Hart's Manufacturing Company on East 20th Street. The Torso Murderer had apparently struck again. Lieutenant Harvey Weitzel responded to the call along with Detective Sergeant James Hogan and Detectives Shibley and Wachsman. Detective Joseph Sweeney later said that police believed the body had been placed behind the factory at around 2:30 A.M., because James Marco, who lived near Hart's, told police that his dog began howling around that time. During the autopsy, Coroner Pearse determined that the headless torso discovered in the basket belonged to a woman who had been dead for at least two days. Like the corpses at Kingsbury Run, she had apparently been dismembered by someone who knew how to cut apart flesh.

Fingerprints taken from the victim's right hand soon allowed police to identify her as forty-two-year-old Florence Polillo, formerly of Buffalo, New York. A friendly woman who bleached her hair red, Polillo—also known as Florence Martin and Clara Dunn—was a prostitute who lived at a rooming house at 3205 Carnegie

Avenue, not far from where her remains were discovered. When the authorities investigated further, they learned that Polillo had been married twice; her second marriage to Andrew Polillo, a forty-year-old postal worker, had lasted about six years when she lived in Buffalo. When Andrew Polillo was questioned by authorities, he told the police that everything had been fine with their marriage until she started to drink and decided to leave him to find a way to get sober. Unfortunately, she instead descended further into the bottle and began drifting from town to town.

The police discovered that Polillo had previously been arrested for prostitution in their city and Washington, D.C. But no one in her wide circle of friends, including local bartenders, drug addicts, and other prostitutes, had any idea of how she had died.

The rest of Polillo's remains, except for her head, were discovered the following week scattered behind a vacant house on Orange Street just a few blocks away from where the rest of her body had been found. Although there were similarities between Polillo and the victims who had been found in Kingsbury Run, Nickel noted "Detective Sergeant James T. Hogan, the newly appointed head of Homicide, refused to acknowledge a parallel to the four-month-old murders of Andrassy and his unknown companion, despite the unusual feature of death by decapitation." Instead, Hogan announced that the Polillo case would be treated as an isolated incident. When the police were unable to obtain any useful evidence that pointed them toward the killer, however, they were once again forced to admit defeat.

In the meantime, Ness continued to effect change within the city's police department, which often resulted in the arrest and conviction of corrupt officers. Mayor Burton was pleased, especially since the city was going to host two important events that year—the Republican National Convention in June and the Cleveland Centennial celebration in July. The convention was important because it would give outsiders a chance to see all of the improvements that the mayor had made since he had taken office. Although the Kingsbury Run case was once again dormant by that time, Ness worked furiously to make sure that the candidates would have a memorable and safe visit. When the delegates began arriving on June 5, they were duly impressed by the beautifully landscaped Public Square, a new city hall, and the classical-style Terminal Tower, which was then one of the tallest buildings in the world. They never actually saw Kingsbury Run, but unfortunately they would soon hear about it. The same weekend that the delegates arrived, another headless corpse was discovered at the ravine.

Two boys, who were on their way to go fishing, instead hooked the latest victim of the Mad Butcher. When police arrived at the Run, they found the remains of a tall, handsome, and clean-shaven young man in his mid-twenties, who had apparently been dead for several days. The coroner determined that, like the other victims, he had been decapitated while he was still alive and then his remains had been moved to the ravine. It was obvious that the young man was not a member of the hobo population, because he was too well-fed. He had six unusual tattoos on his body, including a cupid super-imposed on an anchor, the popular cartoon figure Jiggs, and the initials "W. C. G." A pile of expensive bloodstained clothing was found near the body, along with a pair of underwear marked with the initials "J. D." Like the others, his body had been drained of blood and washed clean; his head was discovered nearby.

Pearse could not ignore the similarities between this latest victim and those who had previously been found at Kingsbury Run, as well as Florence Polillo. And the press apparently agreed. The day before the start of the Republican National Convention, every paper was filled with stories about the return of the maniac who had apparently been terrorizing Cleveland for years. When Eliot Ness met with the officers under his command, he determined that all of the murders were too similar in style not to be the work of one person. Although the police were reluctant to agree, no one was comfortable with the idea of voicing a dissenting opinion to their new boss. Ness instructed his officers to avoid releasing any information to the press, primarily to ensure that the conventioneers would enjoy their visit to Cleveland. At that time, the convention was his first priority, so he didn't see a need to personally supervise the murder investigation.

The detectives were certain that the latest victim would be easy to identify, primarily because of his unusual tattoos. But they had no luck when they checked local bars and tattoo parlors. The fingerprint files also provided no information. A death mask of the "Tattooed Man," as he became known, was placed on exhibit in the police department's pavilion when the Great Lake Exposition opened later that summer. More than ten million visitors attended the event to enjoy amusement park rides and be entertained by celebrities such as Johnny Weismuller and Esther Williams. While many of them gazed with fascination on the face of the "Tattooed Man," no one ever stepped forward to provide him with a name.

As Ness continued to root out corruption in Cleveland's police department, another John Doe was discovered. On July 22, 1936, the police were called after a teenage girl came across the headless corpse of a man near a hobo camp in the rural area known as Big Creek in Brooklyn, on the southwest side of Cleveland. The victim, probably a transient, was a small man about forty years of age with long hair. A worn gray single-breasted suit, along with a shirt, shoes, and undergarments, had been piled neatly next to the badly decomposed body, while his skull lay about fifteen feet away. The coroner determined that the man had probably been dead about two months. Although the victim had not been transported to Kingsbury Run, the detectives finally agreed that he had very likely been killed by the same person responsible for the other murders. The detectives assigned to the case tried to follow Ness's orders to avoid any undue publicity, but the newspapers repeatedly ran stories demanding to know the identity of the madman who was chopping off heads in Cleveland. Once again, the police failed to turn up any clues to the identity of the killer.

Before long, the press turned its attention back to the successful gambling raids that Ness was conducting throughout the city, making a huge dent in the mob's income. But on September 10, 1936, the body of another victim, who had probably been dead for two days, was discovered in Kingsbury Run. According to Nickel, a drifter named Jerry Harris from St. Louis, who had tried to look for work in Cleveland, was preparing to ride the rails out of town when he stumbled over a headless man's torso near the tracks. As hundreds of spectators watched, the police searched the ravine and discovered a torn denim shirt and faded underwear nearby. The coroner determined that the man, brown-haired and in his mid-twenties, had probably weighed about 150 pounds and stood about 5 feet, 9 inches tall. Like the other male victims, his penis had been cut off and his body had been completely drained of blood.

Shortly after this latest discovery, the police created a special twenty-five-man task force, who worked on the cases full time, reviewing past murders and tracking down possible suspects. Although the mayor may have asked Ness to be more actively involved, the director of public safety preferred to focus his attention on internal affairs in the police department. Instead, Ness delegated responsibility for the investigation to his assistant director and veteran officers like Detective Sergeant James Hogan and Detective Peter Merylo and his partner Detective Martin Zalewski. While Cleveland residents began staying home at night behind locked doors, Merylo and Zalewski often prowled the streets dressed as hobos, questioning the transients of Kingsbury Run. Despite their efforts, no progress was made on the case. On September 15, 1936, the Cleveland *Plain Dealer* reported the following:

> Police last night were holding two more men in connection with the torso murders, but Hogan hoped for little from either. One, 31, wanted for a 1923 assault and battery charge, offered himself as a decoy. The other, 52, brought in by Detective Sergeant Peter Allen yesterday, is an admitted pervert.

The following month, Merylo and Zalewski arrested a sixty-year-old man who apparently fit the killer's behavioral profile, as described by criminologists. When the detectives approached him, the man was wearing a wet washcloth beneath three wool caps, despite the intense summer heat. When his pockets were emptied, police discovered that he carried three large pocket knives, three safety razors, a 6-inch homemade stiletto, and a blackjack made from the head of a hammer. Unfortunately, the detectives were later forced to release the man when he could not be connected to the murders.

Cleveland residents undoubtedly breathed a sigh of relief in the months that followed when no further dismembered victims turned up. But the killer wasn't through terrorizing the city yet. The body of a woman was found near Euclid Beach on the shore of Lake Erie on February 23, 1937, in the same spot where the torso of the Lady of the Lake had been discovered. Dr. Samuel Gerber, the new coroner, was unable to determine an exact cause of death, even though the victim had also been beheaded. Merylo and Zalewski scoured the neighborhood without success; they could not identify the woman or find any clues as to who might have killed her. Then, another woman, who was tentatively identified as Rose Wallace, was found beneath the Lorain-Carnegie Bridge on June 6, 1937, by fourteen-year-old Russell Tower, who had spent the morning by the river. There was some doubt about the identification because thirty-five-year-old Wallace had reportedly disappeared from the city ten months earlier and the victim had been dead for at least one year. While the dental records indicated a close match, the dentist who had performed the work had died several years before, so the police were reluctant to confirm that the latest victim was in fact Wallace. But that didn't matter to the residents of Cleveland, who were once again terrified, even though the unknown killer seemed to target only the poor and homeless. The mayor and Ness were loudly criticized by the public and the press for failing to stop the Mad Butcher, who, like Jack the Ripper, seemed to disappear at will.

Life in Cleveland was further disrupted that summer when violence broke out between the labor unions and factory owners. While the police and Ohio National Guard attempted the keep the peace, the killer reclaimed everyone's attention. On July 6 of that year, another man, who had probably been dead for at least two days before his remains were discovered, was found floating in the Cuyahoga River in the Cleveland Flats. Several days passed before all of his body parts, except for his head, were recovered. The coroner determined that he too had been alive when he was decapitated by his killer.

Almost in response to renewed attention from the police, the murders stopped until the following spring when the remains of another woman were found on April 8 in the Cuyahoga River in the same section of the city. Although authorities were unable to identify her, the coroner believed she had been dead for approximately three days when her body parts were found. According to John Boertlein, author of *Ohio Confidential*, the woman had apparently been injected with a massive dose of morphine before she died. But she was not the only new victim. While the next Jane Doe's body was not found until August 16 at the East 9th Street Lakeshore Dump, authorities believed that the unidentified woman had been dead at least four months. That meant she was probably murdered at about the same time as the previous victim. She was not the only victim discovered that day at the dump. The body of an unidentified man, who was believed to have been dead for at least seven months, was also recovered there.

Hoping to frustrate the killer, Ness ordered the shacks at Kingsbury Run to be burned to the ground. He apparently hoped to better control the movements of the hobo population by forcing them to seek shelter at the city's poorhouse. In response, the local press chastised him for what it saw as punishment of the transients instead of a concerted effort to catch the Mad Butcher.

With no leads, no motives, and no more suspects, the police were stumped. Then Dr. Francis E. Sweeney came to their attention. A local physician, Sweeney voluntarily entered into a mental institution in 1938 and suddenly the killings stopped. Ness believed that the doctor chose to be hospitalized in order to avoid prosecution for the murders. Ness felt that Sweeney, a tall, well-muscled man, fit the profile created by the criminologists. Born and raised in the Kingsbury Run area, Sweeney came from a poor family, but had managed to put himself through medical school. Before opening a successful civilian practice, he had worked in a medical unit during World War I. He had conducted amputations on the battlefield but was later discharged after suffering a head injury. Although educated and intelligent, Sweeney eventually became an alcoholic, which destroyed both his marriage and his medical practice. The doctor failed to pass two polygraph tests, but Ness doubted he would be able to successfully bring him to trial. The doctor was the cousin of Congressman Martin L. Sweeney, who had publicly denounced Ness on more than one occasion for not capturing the killer. Dr. Sweeney remained hospitalized until 1965, and during that time, he sent Ness postcards, taunting him for failing to identify the phantom murderer. He died that same year in a veterans' hospital in Dayton.

While Sweeney played cat-and-mouse with Ness, Merylo and Zalewski decided to turn their attention back to the murder of Edward Andrassy, with the hope of finding some overlooked leads. In his book, Nickel stated, "Since Andrassy had been murdered long before anyone realized a serial killer was on the loose, Merylo was convinced that a more extensive investigation at the time would have resulted in the Butcher's capture." Despite their efforts, no additional suspects came to light. When a new suspect did turn up, tensions were running high and some police officers did not feel compelled to search for more than circumstantial evidence. On August 24, 1939, a drifter named Frank Dolezal died under suspicious circumstances at the Cuyahoga County Jail. Arrested as a suspect in Florence Polillo's murder, Dolezal had six broken ribs that his friends claimed occurred after he was arrested the previous month by Sheriff Martin O'Donnell. While the suspect had initially confessed to killing Polillo in self-defense, he later recanted the statement, which he said had been made after a brutal beating by the authorities. Even though the sheriff claimed that Dolezal committed suicide by hanging himself from the bars of his cell, it was likely that the suspect did not kill himself—at least, not without help.

In the case of both Sweeney and Dolezal, no conclusive evidence was ever produced that would allow the police to determine if one of them was the Torso Murderer. While most of the killer's twelve victims were never identified as anything more than John Doe, they all seemed to have been part of the transient subculture that existed just outside the scope of most people's lives. The killer may not have been the most prolific serial killer in America, but then again the final victim count remains unknown. According to Nickel, "The official body count in Cleveland reached twelve, but at least one of the detectives closest to the case maintained that a number of similar killings outside the city were the work of the same man."

Authorities later determined that the Kingsbury Run Killer's victims may have included the unidentified woman known as the Lady of the Lake and also Robert Robertson, whose body was found on July 22, 1950, at a business at 2138 Davenport Avenue. He had apparently been dead for about two months, and, like the other victims, he had been decapitated. If that was true, then it seemed that the killer was secure in the knowledge that the police had never identified him. And no information was available on whether Sweeney was still institutionalized at that time or had been released to the care of his family. Authorities from Pennsylvania later stepped forward to note that headless bodies had been found in swamps there as early as the 1920s. The body of a headless man who was never unidentified was found in a boxcar on July 1, 1936, while three more headless victims were discovered in boxcars near McKee's Rocks, Pennsylvania, on May 3, 1940.

Some later said that the Torso Murderer also killed the detective career of Eliot Ness, who resigned from his position as Cleveland's director of public safety in 1942. He worked briefly in Washington, D.C., before becoming the chairman of Diebold Incorporated, a safe manufacturer in Canton, in 1944. In 1947, he unsuccessfully ran for mayor in Cleveland. This same year, after the Diebold Corporation released Ness from his contract, he took a position with North Ridge Industrial in Pennsylvania. On May 16, 1957, Ness died from a heart attack. After he was cremated, his ashes were returned to

Cleveland and a commemorative marker was placed in his honor at Lake View Cemetery.

Although not as infamous as other serial killers, such as Jack the Ripper and H. H. Holmes, Cleveland's Mad Butcher inspired Steven Nickel's nonfiction account, *Torso,* as well as a novel also called *Torso,* by John Peyton Cooke. Kingsbury Run, which once inspired fear in the residents of Cleveland, was partially filled in and turned into a large park that today is a popular local attraction for both area residents and tourists.

In 1943, the residents of Cleveland were shocked by the brutal rape and murder of five-year-old Mary Jane Brady, who had been abducted from her aunt's apartment on a warm summer night. As frantic relatives began to search, the child's body was soon discovered about 100 feet from the rear of the apartment building. When police arrived on the scene, a quick search of the neighborhood led them to the apartment of Bernice Radloff, the wife of a U.S. serviceman, who was living with thirty-two-year-old Edward Ralph. Described by law enforcement as a psychopath, Ralph had spent most of his childhood in and out of reformatories, including Mansfield, which had a reputation for brutalizing the inmates. Ralph initially declared his innocence, even though his clothing was stained with the girl's blood, but he finally confessed after police elicited testimony from Radloff's six-year-old son, Jimmie. The boy told police that Ralph had brought Mary Jane to their apartment and that he later heard the sounds of a struggle coming from the next room. Ralph, an alcoholic who claimed to suffer blackouts, was executed at 8 P.M. on October 4 of that same year. A little more than a decade later, Cleveland residents would reel from the news of another brutal slaying.

CHAPTER 4
The Real Fugitive

✳ ✳ ✳

Doctors are required to take an oath to protect those in their care from harm. As a result, it was difficult for anyone to believe that a respected Cleveland physician could actually be guilty of murdering his pregnant wife—a case that continues to divide Ohio residents to this day.

By age thirty-one, Samuel Holmes Sheppard enjoyed an excellent reputation as an osteopathic surgeon and an upscale lifestyle in Bay Village, a suburb west of Cleveland. He had a beautiful wife, Marilyn, and a young son, Samuel, nicknamed "Chip." Everything appeared to be fine with the family until the early morning hours of July 4, 1954, when a bushy-haired man allegedly broke into their home. Sheppard, who had fallen asleep downstairs in front of the television the night before, was awakened by a noise and knocked unconscious by an intruder when he went to investigate. The stranger then brutally attacked Marilyn in their upstairs master bedroom. When Sheppard came to, he followed the intruder out of the home, only to be attacked a second time and knocked cold once again. At least, that's what the doctor later told the police.

Tried and convicted of Marilyn's murder, Sheppard served ten years in prison before he was released after a second trial. But "Doctor Sam," as he was known throughout the close-knit community of Bay Village, would never recapture his glory days. He slid into alcoholism and depression and took the truth of what happened that fateful night with him when he died at age forty-six on April 6, 1970.

Sheppard was born on December 29, 1923, to Richard and Ethel Sheppard, who lived in the upper-income suburbs of Cleveland, an area known as Cleveland Heights. Richard, a doctor of osteopathic medicine, was an ambitious man who saw no reason why his family shouldn't build a medical dynasty in Ohio. At the time, many doctors frowned upon the practice of osteopathy, which believed that all disease could be treated by manipulating the spine. Sheppard's father expanded that foundation to include other forms of treatment and before long was running his own hospital, where osteopathy was an accepted discipline. The youngest of three boys, Samuel Sheppard was good-looking but lacked his father's ambition. He dreamed of becoming a professional athlete but soon learned that he was expected, like his brothers Richard Jr. and Steven, to follow in his father's footsteps and become a doctor of osteopathic medicine.

Sheppard and Marilyn Reese were high school sweethearts whose relationship was briefly interrupted in 1941 when she went off to Skidmore College in New York. Highly intelligent, Marilyn was also homesick and in love, so she dropped out of college after her freshman year to work and wait for Sheppard to finish college. The couple married shortly after he graduated from the Los Angeles Osteopathic School of Physicians in September 1945. They lived on an allowance from his father and on what Marilyn earned as a part-time lab assistant while Sheppard finished an internship that resulted in a Doctor of Osteopathy degree in 1948. Encouraged by their parents, the couple decided it was time to start a family, but Marilyn's first pregnancy was difficult for her; she experienced postpartum depression after the baby was born. To cheer her up, Sheppard sent Marilyn and Chip to Cleveland to visit her family for a few weeks, but his motives were not entirely altruistic. While she was away, Sheppard went on several dates with nurses—starting a pattern that he would repeat with regularity throughout their married life. According to James Neff, author of *The Wrong Man: The Final Verdict on the Dr. Sam Sheppard Murder Case*, even after Marilyn returned "Sam had had several affairs, one with the wife of a resident doctor on staff at Los Angeles County General Hospital, another with a nursing instructor." Interestingly enough, he often told Marilyn about these relationships, assuring her that they were nothing more than casual flings.

Marilyn began to believe that she was sexually frigid because she did not share Sheppard's apparent appetite for sex on a daily basis. Although she was upset by his behavior, she wasn't about to walk away from her marriage, for two reasons: divorce carried a strong social stigma at the time and she felt a part of her was still in love with her handsome husband. But when her husband's flirting embarrassed her at a hospital function one night, Marilyn returned to Cleveland to enlist the help of Sheppard's entire family. Her in-laws rallied to her side and advised their youngest to grow up, act like a married man, and start shouldering his responsibilities.

In the weeks that followed, the Sheppards both made a concerted effort to repair their relationship and decided that a change of scenery would probably help. In 1951, with four-year-old Chip in tow, they returned to the Buckeye State. Sheppard was going to work with his father and two brothers at Bay View Hospital on Lake Road in Bay Village. The private, 110-bed facility was owned and operated by the Sheppards, who earned both praise and criticism for their innovative medical treatment methods. But while many residents of Bay Village considered the family of physicians to be an asset to their small community, a number of doctors felt their constant advertising and press releases in the newspapers was an embarrassment to the medical profession.

The couple bought a house at 28924 Lake Road that sat on a bluff overlooking Lake Erie just down the street from the hospital. While Sheppard went off to work each morning, Marilyn focused on raising their son and keeping house. She taught Bible classes at the Methodist Church they attended each Sunday, and with Sheppard, she enjoyed bowling, tennis, water skiing, and other outdoor sports. On the surface, the couple seemed to have the perfect marriage, but that was far from true. Marilyn was growing increasingly resentful of the long hours her husband spent at the hospital, especially after she learned about his affair with a nurse named Susan Hayes. In the past, Sheppard had mentioned "dates" with other women, but Marilyn had never considered anyone a threat—until now. In the summer of 1954, she was pregnant with their second child and still not ready to give up on her marriage.

On the evening of July 3, the Sheppards enjoyed a quiet dinner at their home with their friends, Don and Nancy Ahern, who lived nearby. The two couples spent a lot of time together, often going bowling or dancing. That night, they watched a movie on television until about midnight. Then the Aherns gathered up their children and went home. After they left, Sheppard fell asleep on a day bed in the living room while Marilyn went upstairs. Nancy Ahern later told the police she couldn't remember if Marilyn had locked the door behind them.

Sheppard later said that he was awakened by a noise in the middle of the night. Was it Marilyn calling his name? He raced up the stairs to see a light-colored form in front of him grappling with his wife. Before he could intervene, Sheppard told the police he was struck from behind and collapsed to the floor. When he came to, he saw his wife's body, covered in blood, lying prone on the bed. He immediately checked her pulse, only to find that Marilyn was dead. Sheppard rushed to his son's bedroom and was relieved to find Chip safe and fast asleep. He heard a noise from the first floor, the doctor said, and ran downstairs to find the back door of their home standing open. He saw a man he later described as about six foot, three inches in height, middle-aged, with dark bushy hair, running toward the lake. Sheppard chased the intruder across his backyard and down to the beach, where they fought briefly before Sheppard was knocked unconscious a second time. Sheppard later said he had no idea how long he was out before he stumbled back to his house. Climbing the stairs, he once again was confronted by the nightmare scene of his wife's brutal death. Authorities later determined that Marilyn had apparently been beaten so badly that two of her teeth were missing. In his book, Neff stated, "She was unrecognizable. About two dozen deep, ugly crescent-shaped gashes marked her face, forehead, and scalp." In addition, Marilyn's pajama top had been pushed up to expose her breasts, and her pajama bottoms had been pulled down.

Despite his affiliation with the local police department as the doctor who handled emergency cases, Sheppard did not immediately call any officers to the scene. Instead, at about five o'clock that morning, he telephoned his friend and neighbor, Spencer Houk, the mayor of Bay Village. Houk and his wife Esther, who lived just two doors away, hurried over to the Sheppard home. The mayor called the police about an hour later. After Officer Fred Drenkhan arrived at the scene, he realized that the village's small police department was not equipped to handle a murder investigation. Although he had been on the force for about three years, Drenkhan's experience primarily involved writing tickets for traffic violations and investigating the occasional burglary.

Two detectives, Robert Schottke and Patrick Gareau, were sent out from Cleveland to assist the local police. Veteran investigators who had worked together for about seven years, the detectives were appalled at what they found when they arrived at the scene. Not only were friends and neighbors trampling through the Sheppards' yard, destroying possible clues, they were also handling objects like the doctor's medical bag, which had been discovered in the backyard. According to John Boertlein, author of *Ohio Confidential*, "Inside the bag were Dr. Sam's wristwatch, fraternity ring from Hanover College, and his keys." Schottke and Gareau did not agree with local authorities that a drug addict had broken into the Sheppard home. Nor did they believe that Marilyn had been sexually assaulted by an intruder. From the beginning, they considered Dr. Sam to be the prime suspect, and they were not the only ones who were quickly convinced of his guilt.

Dr. Samuel Gerber, the veteran medical coroner who had worked on the unsolved Kingsbury Run murders, had decided almost immediately that the doctor was responsible for his wife's death. Gerber's perspective, however, may have been colored by his dislike for the entire Sheppard family, because he was one of the doctors who did not consider osteopathy to be a legitimate form of medical treatment. Arriving at the scene at about eight o'clock, Gerber found it difficult to believe Sheppard's account of what had happened, as related to him by Drenkhan. Although drawers had been pulled out of a desk in the living room, the entire scene was a little too neat to satisfy the veteran coroner.

While the detectives were still at the crime scene, Gerber went to the hospital to examine Sheppard and collect the clothing he had worn earlier that day. After he returned to the Sheppard house, the coroner conferred with Schottke and Gareau, and according to Neff, "Gerber and the detectives agreed that it looked as if someone had staged a burglary." When they finished with their interviews at the house, Schottke and Gareau confronted Sheppard later that same morning as he was getting his wounds treated at the hospital. Among other things, the detectives wanted to know why there was no evidence of any forced entry into the house and why no one heard the Sheppards' dog—always on the alert for strangers—bark that night.

Sheppard, hospitalized with a fractured vertebra and chipped teeth, could not satisfactorily answer their questions. Schottke and Gareau also found it difficult to believe that the doctor had been knocked unconscious twice in one night. If he saw an intruder when he first climbed the stairs, how was he struck from behind? Was there a second person involved? But Sheppard's brother, Steven, who was also his personal physician, kept interrupting the detectives during the interview and finally demanded that they leave so his patient could rest.

The police investigation continued into the following day. At one point, the detectives from Cleveland theorized that the murder might have been committed by the doctor as a crime of passion. Was it possible that Marilyn had been unfaithful to Sheppard and was pregnant with another man's child? They soon learned from Nancy Ahern that while men flirted with Marilyn, she was not the one with the wandering eye. Ahern told them about Sheppard's ongoing infidelities, notably his three-year affair with Susan Hayes, who no longer worked at Bay View Hospital. After several more days of reviewing the evidence, the detectives from Cleveland advised Bay Village police that Sheppard should be considered the prime suspect in Marilyn's murder. Bay Village authorities remained reluctant, however, to arrest such a prominent, well-respected member of the community.

As the doctor's wife was laid to rest on July 7 at Knollwood Cemetery, Schottke and Gareau, together with officers from the county sheriff's department, searched the Sheppard home once again. According to Neff, "This time, detectives picked up some physical evidence that they had ignored or missed the days before or perhaps had been inadvertently dropped there by photographers, reporters, or police who had been in the house." As the lake was dredged for a possible murder weapon, the officers found a chip of red paint and a small piece of leather inside the house.

The following day, as Sheppard still lay hospitalized, Gerber voiced his displeasure with the case to the media. He had tried to subpoena the entire Sheppard family, but Sheppard's attorney, William Corrigan, resisted the coroner's plan. The counsel for the defense, however, had underestimated Gerber's determination to have Dr. Sam arrested. The coroner told the newspapers that both he and the police did not believe a drug addict had broken into the Sheppard home. And Gerber also questioned why Sheppard had waited for more than an hour to call for assistance. In the meantime, public opinion, fueled by newspaper editorials, soon turned against the doctor when it seemed that his public demonstrations of grief were staged rather than genuine. In response, Sheppard offered a $10,000 reward for information leading to the arrest of his wife's killer. Unfortunately, his offer did little to appease the public or the local papers.

On July 11, pathologist Mary Cowan was brought to the Sheppard home by Gerber to examine a variety of blood samples and fibers collected at the scene. Cowan, a protégé of the coroner, was one of the first women in Ohio to work in field of pathology. She later testified that not all of her tests were conclusive. Although Marilyn's blood appeared to be present on both her own wristwatch and that of her husband, Cowan could not state that Sheppard's

CAPITAL PUNISHMENT
IN THE BUCKEYE STATE

Like all states, Ohio used capital punishment on a regular basis after it first joined the Union in 1803. For close to one hundred years, public hangings took place in the county where the crime was committed. But in 1885, the state legislature passed a law that required all executions were to take place at the Ohio Penitentiary in Columbus. Valentine Wagner, fifty-six, was the first person to be executed at the penitentiary. The Morrow County resident was hanged for the murder of Daniel Shehan of Mount Gilead. Twenty-seven other convicted murderers were later hanged at the prison.

In 1897, the gallows was replaced by a modern marvel, the electric chair, which was believed to be a more humane form of execution. The first prisoner to be executed in the chair was seventeen-year-old William blood was present as well. Neither could she match the red fibers taken from beneath the victim's fingernails as belonging to any clothing or carpeting in the Sheppard home. Forensic science was still in its infancy at that time, but some questions were later raised about Cowan's findings. Had she really been unable to establish any firm evidence or had she simply misrepresented her findings to please her mentor?

In the weeks that followed, the media demanded to know why no inquest had been held. By the end of July, the auditorium of Normandy Elementary School was selected as the only site large enough for the inquest, which attracted both the public and the press. Local papers were quick to disseminate some of the more sordid details of the case, especially after Susan Hayes was subpoenaed to testify. She told the court that her affair with Dr. Sam had started in May 1951, almost immediately after the Sheppards moved to Cleveland. But about three years later, Hayes ended their tumultuous relationship, finally realizing that Sheppard was never going to divorce his wife.

Haas of Hamilton County for the murder of Mrs. William Brady. Between 1897 and 1963, 312 men and 3 women died in the electric chair. The final inmate to be executed by electrocution on March 15, 1963, was Donald Reinbolt, a twenty-nine-year-old inmate from Franklin County, for the murder of Edgar L. Weaver, a Columbus grocer.

After the United States Supreme Court declared the death penalty to be unconstitutional in 1972, the sentences of sixty-five inmates on death row were commuted to life in prison. That same year, the penitentiary's death row was moved to the Southern Ohio Correctional Facility at Lucasville. Although the Ohio General Assembly tried to revise the state's death penalty law two years later, the U.S. Supreme Court rejected their attempt in 1978. As a result, 116 male prisoners and 4 female inmates had their sentences commuted to life in prison.

(continued on page 60)

> But Ohio legislators apparently were not ready to concede that the death penalty should no longer be used. In 1981, they enacted the current capital punishment statute, which allows it to be used in certain cases. Although Leonard Jenkins of Cuyahoga County was the first to be sentenced under the current law, his sentence and those of three other men and four women were later commuted to life by Gov. Richard Celeste in 1991. Seven of the eight pardons were later deemed by the Franklin County Common Pleas Court to have been improperly imposed and the death penalty was reinstated for those inmates. They were returned to death row in 1992, but that decision was overturned five years later after

She moved to California to get away from him, but they renewed their affair when he returned to the West Coast for some advanced medical training.

Despite the apparent motives that had come to light during the inquest, the police in Bay Village still dragged their feet about arresting Sheppard. It wasn't until officials in Cleveland threatened to remove Schottke and Gareau from the investigation that the doctor was taken into custody by the local police on July 29. Lead prosecutor John J. Mahon, who was then running for a seat on the Cuyahoga County Court of Common Pleas, was reportedly pleased to be involved with the high-profile case, which he felt would help him win him the election. During the trial, the prosecution revealed Sheppard's longstanding relationship with Hayes, which according to the state was sufficient motive for the doctor to have killed his wife.

The Sheppard family had hired Corrigan, one of the best-known attorneys in Cleveland, to defend the doctor. That strategy backfired when the press and the public questioned why Dr. Sam, if he was innocent, needed such a high-profile defense lawyer. When Corrigan addressed the jury, he noted the doctor had suffered a number of injuries, including spinal and neck lacerations that had been inflicted by the intruder. Corrigan also argued that if Sheppard had killed Marilyn, his clothing would have been noticeably stained it was challenged in a suit filed by the Ohio attorney general. In the end, the life sentences were reinstated for the seven prisoners.

In 1993, prisoners on death row were given the choice between lethal injection or death by electrocution, in a bill that was passed by Gov. George Voinovich. Six years later, an inmate named Wilford Berry became the first inmate to be executed in Ohio since 1963. Berry was serving a death sentence out of Cuyahoga County for the 1989 murder of Charles Mitroff. He voluntarily waived all of his appeals and selected lethal injection as the method of execution.

with her blood. He conveniently left out the lapse in time before the police were called when the doctor could have washed and changed his clothes.

When Sheppard took the stand, he told the jury that he had been sleeping downstairs when he heard his wife screaming. After racing upstairs, only to be knocked out, he found Marilyn was already dead when he regained consciousness. Corrigan called more than a dozen character witnesses to the stand to speak on the doctor's behalf after Sheppard finished with his testimony. Two witnesses testified that they had in fact seen a bushy-haired man loitering near the Sheppard home on the day of the crime.

The jury was apparently not persuaded, because on December 21, Sheppard was convicted of second-degree murder and immediately sentenced to life at the Ohio State Prison in Columbus. His supporters would later argue that Sheppard had been tried and convicted in the media long before he ever appeared in court.

Reeling from the verdict, the Sheppard family would soon face further tragedy: About two weeks after his conviction, Sheppard's mother committed suicide and his father died after a gastric ulcer hemorrhaged. During the ten years behind bars that followed, Sheppard spent countless hours appealing his sentence. His story even caught the attention of Erle Stanley Gardner, author of the Perry

Mason novels, who related Sheppard's case in his column, "The Court of Last Resort," which ran in *Argosy* magazine. According to the authors of *Crimes of the 20th Century*, Gardner noted that Paul Leland Kirk, a criminology professor at the University of California, thoroughly examined the scene of the crime and "discovered that the state had suppressed evidence found in the murder room of a blood type that belonged neither to Sheppard nor his wife."

After Corrigan died, the Sheppard family hired an up-and-coming attorney named F. Lee Bailey to represent the inmate. Bailey used Kirk's findings to file further appeals; although his initial efforts were rejected, a United States district court judge granted a petition for a writ of habeaus corpus on July 15, 1964. The judge found that Sheppard's constitutional rights had been violated five times during his trial, and according to www.trutv.com, "the judge said the trial was a mockery of justice." His decision meant that the State of Ohio either had to grant Sheppard a new trial or release him from jail. Ohio authorities opted to let him go—for the moment.

Three days after his release, Sheppard married Ariane Tebbenjohanns, a rich blonde divorcee from Germany who had corresponded with him during his term in prison. But their happiness was short-lived; in May 1965, the federal appeals court reinstated Sheppard's conviction and the following year, a second trial was held. In this trial, neither Sheppard nor Susan Hayes took the stand, a strategy that proved to be successful when a verdict of not guilty was returned by the jury on November 16.

Sheppard undoubtedly had every hope of resuming the type of life he had enjoyed before Marilyn's murder. He moved to Youngstown and immediately returned to practicing medicine, and co-authored the book *Endure and Conquer*, which presented his side of the case and told the story of his life in prison. But was there some residual guilt lingering inside him? Dr. Sam's practice soon declined as he became addicted to alcohol and drugs. Before long, he was sued for malpractice when one of his patients died. Finally, just four years after they were married, the second Mrs. Sheppard divorced him on October 7, 1969, after she claimed he had stolen money from her and threatened her with physical violence.

With his life once more in shambles, Sheppard decided to try his skill as a professional wrestler, using a "nerve hold" that he perfected. Although no one really knows why he chose such a dramatic career change, he became known as "The Killer" and wrestled with partner George Strickland in matches across the United States. In 1969, he reportedly married his wrestling manager's twenty-year-old daughter, but no records of the marriage have ever been located.

But it seemed that success and happiness would escape his grasp once again. Sheppard died of liver failure on April 6, 1970. Buried in Forest Lawn Memorial Gardens in Columbus, his body was exhumed in 1997 for DNA testing, as part of the lawsuit brought by his son to clear his name. After the tests, the body was cremated and the ashes were placed in a mausoleum at Knollwood Cemetery in Mayfield Heights with those of his first wife, Marilyn.

Sheppard's story later inspired the television series and film, both titled *The Fugitive*, about a wrongfully convicted man who seeks his wife's killer. Although Neff concluded that the doctor was not guilty of the crime, law enforcement officials, despite the opinion of the courts, still believed he was responsible for Marilyn's death. In 1999, Gregg McCrary, the FBI's Supervisory Special Agent with the Behavioral Science Unit, was asked to review the Sheppard case. Using his skills as a criminal profiler, gained in working cases throughout the United States, McCrary determined that the crime scene at the Sheppard home contained elements of "staging." That meant someone purposefully tried to alter the scene to hide his true motive for committing murder. In this case, McCrary noted that the killer tried to make it seem as though Marilyn was not his primary target. But like any amateur, the person was not completely successful in masking his real intentions. The veteran investigator, with more than thirty years of experience, added that while the house appeared to have been ransacked, there were too many inconsistencies at the scene for him to believe the intruder had been after drugs or money. Neither had Marilyn been the victim of a sexual assault, despite the partial removal of her pajamas.

That same year, Samuel Reese Sheppard sued the State of Ohio in the Cuyahoga County Court of Common Pleas for his father's wrongful imprisonment. To determine if jealousy had played a role in her murder, the court ordered Marilyn's body to be exhumed to see if her unborn child had possibly been fathered by another man. Unfortunately, there was too much formaldehyde in the tissue to determine the paternity of the baby.

Terry Gilbert, who had been retained to represent the Sheppard family, proposed another possible theory. He told the court that a handyman named Richard Eberling might have been guilty of the crime. Eberling had worked on occasion at the Sheppard home and one of Marilyn's rings had allegedly been later found in his possession. Unfortunately for the Sheppards, Eberling had died the preceding year in an Ohio prison, where he was serving a life sentence for the 1984 murder of Ethel May Durkin, an elderly, wealthy widow from Lakewood.

Durkin had no immediate family, so she had appointed Eberling as her guardian and executor of her will. The handyman became a suspect in her murder after a court-appointed review of the woman's estate revealed that he had failed to execute her final wishes regarding her burial. After Durkin's body was exhumed, authorities discovered additional injuries during an autopsy that did not match Eberling's previous claim that she had died as the result of an accidental fall down a staircase in her home. When the police investigated further, they found that both of Durkin's sisters, Myrtle Fray and Sarah Belle Farrow, had also died under suspicious circumstances, but once again, no one could determine if Eberling was involved. The handyman and his partner, Obie Henderson, were found guilty in Durkin's death, but a DNA test of Eberling's blood—to see if it matched the blood samples found at the Sheppard home—was inconclusive.

Though Eberling had previously denied any involvement in Marilyn's murder, a fellow convict reported that the handyman had confessed to the crime. Kathie Collins Dyal, a home healthcare worker for Durkin, also testified that Eberling had confessed to her in 1983. But the credibility of both witnesses was seriously called into question during the 2000 civil trial. F. Lee Bailey, Sheppard's attorney during his 1966 retrial, insisted in his testimony in the 2000 civil lawsuit that Eberling could not have been the killer. Instead, he suggested that Esther Houk, wife of Bay Village mayor Spencer Houk, had killed Marilyn in a fit of jealous rage after finding out that Marilyn and her husband had an affair.

Cuyahoga County Prosecutor William Mason refused to accept these alternative theories. As far as the State of Ohio was concerned, Marilyn's murder was a domestic homicide, which meant that her husband was the only viable suspect. According to the prosecutor, Sheppard was not happy about his wife's pregnancy because he feared it would have an impact on his extramarital affairs. But with the Sheppards' social position in Bay Village, divorce was out of the question, so he chose murder instead. Questions were raised once again about the lapse in time before the doctor had called for help and why the family dog had not barked if an intruder had entered the house.

After ten weeks of trial, seventy-six witnesses, and hundreds of exhibits, the case went to the eight-person jury, which determined on April 12, 2000, after three hours of deliberation, that Samuel Reese Sheppard had failed to prove his father had been wrongfully imprisoned. Two years later, the Eighth District Court of Appeals ruled unanimously that the civil case should not have gone to the jury because a wrongful imprisonment claim could be made only by the person actually imprisoned and not by a family member. Later that same year, the Supreme Court of Ohio affirmed the appeals court's decision. While the Sheppard case might now be considered legally resolved, it remains a highly controversial subject in the Cleveland area. And while Samuel Reese Sheppard was unable to succeed in clearing his father's name, in 2010 he continued to fight for causes like the abolition of the death penalty through Journey of Hope, an organization that he cofounded.

Sheppard was an inmate at the Ohio State Prison in Columbus on October 31, 1952, when some of the prisoners decided to stage what would later become known as the "Halloween Riot." Like many prisons throughout the United States at that time, the Ohio facility was overcrowded and underfunded, which led to poor food and even worse living conditions. The inmates at the Ohio State Prison apparently rioted that day because they were unhappy with the quality of their dinner. After several prisoners began banging on their cups with spoons in one cafeteria, inmates in another began throwing their food, utensils, and trays. Warden R. W. Alvis made an effort to control the situation, but he and the guards were soon overwhelmed. Although many prisoners chose to go back to their cells, some roamed the corridors and attacked other prisoners. A group of inmates broke into the infirmary in search of drugs, while others set some of the buildings on fire.

About five hours after the riot began, most prisoners were forcibly returned to their cells by a combined force that included the prison guards, Ohio State Highway Patrol officers, city police officers from Columbus, and National Guardsmen. But not all of them were ready to give up. For the next three days, prisoners in cell blocks G, H, I, and K remained loose. Finally, when the authorities cut off their heat and food supplies, the inmates began throwing objects out of their cell block windows. In response, the police opened fire and before the day ended, one inmate was killed and four others were wounded. After the shootings, the remaining inmates surrendered and returned to their cells.

CHAPTER 5
Most Wanted

Bank robbers are usually happy to maintain a low profile, realizing that the less the authorities know about them and their activities, the better. But one Akron man decided that he wasn't content for the media to document his life of crime in an occasional news report. At first opportunity, he wrote his autobiography to tell the world his story.

In August 2009, Edward Wayne Edwards was arraigned in Louisville, Kentucky, for the murder of a young couple in Jefferson County, Wisconsin, that had occurred nearly thirty years earlier. Charged with two counts of first-degree murder, seventy-six-year-old Edwards pleaded not guilty to killing Tim Hack of Hebron and Kelly Drew of Fort Atkinson, nineteen-year-old high school sweethearts who had expected to marry someday. Edwards, who had lived in Louisville for a number of years prior to his arrest, had spent many years behind bars, but he claimed that he had earned his keep as a con man and a bank robber, not a murderer. If anyone doubted

him, the details were all documented in his autobiography, titled
Metamorphosis of a Criminal: The True Life Story of Ed Edwards.

Reportedly suffering from diabetes, leukemia, and heart ailments
and breathing with the help of an oxygen tank, Edwards was confined to a wheelchair when he appeared in court on the murder
charges. Anyone who saw him that day would have had difficulty
believing that he was once on the FBI's ten most wanted fugitives list
or that he had smooth-talked countless women into accompanying
him on his crime sprees. During his arraignment, Edwards told the
court that he was not involved in the deaths of Hack and Drew, who
had disappeared from a wedding reception at the Concord House in
rural Ixonia, Wisconsin, on August 9, 1980. Family members and
friends began to worry when the couple failed to show up in Fort
Atkinson after the reception. Although they had been seen leaving
the party at about eleven o'clock that night, Hack's 1977 brown
Oldsmobile was still in the Concord House parking lot the following day with his jacket and a wallet containing $67 locked inside.

Hack had worn brown pants, a brown shirt, and suede shoes to
the wedding, and Drew, dressed in yellow slacks and a yellow plaid
blouse, had carried a beige macramé purse. Hack's father, David,
contacted the Jefferson County Sheriff's Office the day after the
reception, but it wasn't until later in the week that investigators
found some of Drew's clothing scattered about three miles away
from the Concord House. A pair of women's yellow pants and a
beige bra, according to authorities, apparently had been "cut in a
jagged pattern with a sharp object." Beige bikini underpants found
farther down the road were cut in a similar fashion.

Witnesses reported seeing Edwards with a bloody nose the weekend the couple disappeared, an injury that he claimed had occurred
while he was deer hunting. Working at the time as a handyman at the
Concord House and the adjacent Concord Center Campgrounds,
Edwards was questioned by the sheriff's officers during the course
of their investigation. Shortly afterward, he packed up his family and
disappeared without leaving a forwarding address; the family drifted
for a time from state to state before finally settling in Kentucky.

On October 19, 1980, hunters found the remains of a person about eight miles from Concord House, and another body was discovered the following day. Unfortunately, with limited scientific technology available at the time, the physical evidence did not provide the authorities with many clues. They were able to determine that the two bodies were Hack and Drew. Although Hack had apparently been stabbed to death, it was believed that Drew had been strangled and sexually assaulted. Authorities had no idea, however, who might have committed such a heinous crime or why anyone would want to hurt the young couple. Hack was a farmer who enjoyed spending his free time with Drew, a recent beauty school graduate who had just accepted her first job at a salon.

Although the investigation remained unsolved for decades, dedicated officers, still determined to find the couple's killer, periodically reviewed the file in hope of finding an overlooked clue. When a joint cold case investigation was authorized by the Wisconsin Department of Justice and the Jefferson County Sheriff's Office in 2009, the case was one of the first to be considered. Investigators announced that new information on the case had come to light. A sample of Edwards's DNA was discovered when stains found on Drew's clothing were analyzed at the State Crime Lab at Madison. Armed with a warrant, Wisconsin police arrived at Edwards's door to charge him with the killings. He was extradited from Kentucky to Wisconsin in July 2009. Held in Louisville on $500,000 bail, he faced life in prison if convicted on two counts of first-degree murder. But despite the scientific evidence, he was not going to confess to the crime. Edwards reportedly admitted to detectives that while he had thought about killing people in the past, he had never actually murdered anyone.

Although he had initially denied any knowledge of the crimes when he was first interviewed after his arrest in 2009, the Associated Press reported that Edwards later admitted to Wisconsin authorities "he had sex with the woman and then watched a group of men stomp the couple to death," but never said anything because he "didn't want to get involved." Edwards, who claimed he had been drinking with the couple, said he had consensual sex with Drew in a field near the campground and that was why his DNA had been present on her clothing.

Edwards's bail was later raised to $2 million, because he was considered a flight risk, despite his health concerns. Unable to post bail, the suspect was still behind bars in February 2010, when his defense attorney, Jeffrey De La Rosa, argued for a change of venue. De La Rosa did not believe that the former bank robber would get a fair trial in Jefferson County, but Jefferson County District Attorney Susan Happ contested the proposed change. Circuit Court judge William Hue agreed with Happ and set a trial date for that June.

Interestingly enough, while Edwards pointed to his autobiography as evidence that he had changed his criminal ways, in the book he actually seems to spend a lot of time congratulating himself on always being able to outsmart authorities during the 1950s and '60s, the height of his criminal career. Unfortunately, like Joseph Kallinger and Ernest Ingenito, his story was often the only side accepted as the truth because his victims were not always able to speak for themselves.

According to Edwards, he was born Charles Murray on June 14, 1933, in Akron. His unmarried mother, Lillian Myers, was twenty when he was born, and up until he was sixteen, Edwards was taught that Lillian was his aunt. In 1934, she was sentenced to serve at least one year at the Marysville Reformatory for Women because she was convicted of stealing $100 from her employer while working as a housekeeper. Released on parole the following year, Lillian was unable to adjust to life in the outside world, and according to Edwards, she fatally shot herself in the stomach with a shotgun shortly after she got out of jail.

Young Charles was adopted soon afterward by Mary and Fred Edwards and was rechristened Edward Wayne Edwards. But any hope of a stable home life disappeared after Mary developed multiple sclerosis, an incurable disease that attacks the brain and spinal cord. Mary worried about providing her adopted son with adequate care, because Fred had a drinking problem; so in 1940, she sent seven-year-old Edwards to a Catholic orphanage in Parma. Run by the Sisters of Charity, the facility included twelve cottages, a school, a gym, a dining hall, and a church. There were also baseball and football fields and a swimming pool for the young residents.

Despite all of the amenities at the orphanage, Edwards recalled that he was overwhelmed by the harsh conditions he encountered there. A bedwetter, he stated that he was once forced to endure physical punishment approved by Sister Agnes Marie, the nun in charge of his cottage: "She instructed the children to form a line; and each, in turn, would kick me on the backside, and then return to the end of the line." Edwards estimated that he was probably kicked about two hundred times that day. In response, he ran away, but he was soon hauled back and beaten for leaving. Undeterred, Edwards made fifteen more escape attempts during the next four years and was severely punished each time he was returned.

By that time, orphanage officials were ready to wash their hands of the boy. Repeated psychological testing had shown he was of borderline intelligence and they saw little hope that he would ever conform to their standards. In the meantime, Edwards grew increasingly resentful of what he saw as an organization of hypocrites. He periodically announced to anyone who would listen that he was going to become a master criminal someday. Expelled from the institution in 1945 while in the sixth grade, Edwards went back to Akron to live with his adopted grandmother and his adopted mother, where he attended public school when he felt like it. At twelve, he was already more interested in finding new places to rob, and he begged for money from anyone he thought he could fool. At one point, he even told his neighbors that his grandmother had died and he was collecting money for flowers for her funeral.

In his book, Edwards stated that he soon earned a reputation as a street fighter: "With my inner rage always at a boiling point, I was indeed uncontrollable." When Mary Edwards, who had been bedridden for the final three years of her life, died on October 3, 1945, Edwards made an apparent effort to change his ways. He got a job at a bowling alley as a pin setter and brought most of his salary of

$20 a week home to his grandmother. But before long, he began stealing again and, just for fun, started calling in false alarms to the police and fire departments.

Unable to discipline Edwards, his grandmother readily turned him over to the juvenile authorities at the end of 1947. Although he could have easily wound up at Mansfield, a notorious reformatory in Ohio where young inmates were often abused, he was sent instead to a Catholic-run home called the Philadelphia Protectory for Boys in Montgomery County, Pennsylvania. The facility had been established by the church in 1898 for boys ages eight to fifteen. According to William Henry Slingerland, author of *Child Welfare Work in Pennsylvania*, most of the residents had been committed there by the courts for "various degrees of waywardness." The fourteen-year-old was told that his new home was not a reformatory but a fresh start—a place where he could learn a trade and find a better future.

Eager to move on to new surroundings, Edward was happy to go. But when he stood in front of the three-story yellow brick building, where the dormitories were located, Edwards realized with a sinking feeling that this new school—almost four hundred miles from home—might not be much of an improvement over the orphanage.

Edwards said that during his stay he witnessed the guards making sexual advances on some of the boys and incidents of cruelty among other inmates. To protect himself from the guards and other students, he said he fought at every opportunity. After a year, he was permitted to work on a dairy farm outside of the protectory's grounds. Frantic for a chance to escape, Edwards stated, "One morning, while on my way to milk the cows, I dashed around the back of the barn and headed for the woods. Then, coming out of the woods, I ran onto some railroad tracks, and just sat there, anxiously waiting for a train to come by." Fortunately for him, a freight train bound for Akron soon passed. Edwards hopped onboard and headed west to his hometown.

Knowing that his relatives might report him to the authorities, he kept out of sight for about two weeks, but his penchant for trouble soon surfaced. After he repeatedly charged clothing and food on his family's accounts at different businesses, he was arrested by the police and returned to the protectory. In March 1950, he was released into his grandmother's custody, but the unruly sixteen-year-old once again proved he had no interest in changing his ways. Edwards stole bicycles, money, cars, and anything he could get his hands on. He soon wound up in jail, where his idea of rehabilitation involved sneaking into the women's side at night to have sex with some of the teenage inmates.

After he was released, seventeen-year-old Edwards decided to join the Marines. Following eight weeks of grueling basic training at Parris Island, South Carolina, he was thrilled to don his new uniform and even more excited at the prospect of going overseas. War had just broken out in Korea, but Edwards soon lost interest in the military when he learned a federal law had been passed that prohibited seventeen-year-olds from going into combat. He went AWOL, sewing stolen medals onto his uniform to impress women and con business owners into hiring him so that he could steal cash or merchandise. Before long, Edwards was caught and dishonorably discharged, a fact that ironically worked in his favor when he wound up in jail in Jacksonville, Florida, a short time later. Although Edwards faced the possibility of serving at least five years for car theft and breaking and entering, the judge decided that a dishonorable discharge from the Marines was punishment enough. Instead, he handed Edwards a five-year suspended sentence.

This lucky break boosted his self-confidence. Edwards was soon on the road and creating a new life story for every potential employer he thought he could fool, once again pulling up stakes after stealing as much as he could. Chameleon-like, he was a car salesman, then a food store manager, and at one point even posed as a psychologist. When times were tough, he wrote bad checks and stole auto parts.

Edwards rarely traveled alone; it seemed that he was almost always able to persuade some hapless young woman to accompany him on his travels. Holding out the promise of marriage, Edwards often used them as pawns in his con games. He eventually did marry at least four times, but he noted that one marriage ended in an annulment and another in divorce. He even abandoned one wife in Texas on their wedding night; Edwards wrote that he married Peggy, a Houston woman, on a Saturday afternoon only to take her car later that night and run off to Jacksonville, Florida, with another woman named Donna. He claimed to have had at least five children. There did come a time when Edwards said he got bored with traveling, so he and a companion stopped in Idaho Falls, Idaho, to find work. But as always, any plans he made for settling down were soon replaced by another scheme and another woman.

In March 1952, he was arrested in Philadelphia after he was stopped by police for driving a stolen car while he was wearing a Marine uniform. He was sentenced to two years in the Chillicothe Federal Reformatory in Ross County, south of Hopewell Culture National Historic Park. Edwards admitted in his book that for the first time in his life, he was worried about going to jail because he had no clue what life would be like inside a federal prison. The following month, he was escorted to the reformatory by two federal marshals. He recalled, "I was awed by its size; from the outside, it resembled a small city." His contempt for authority and his fellow prisoners quickly resurfaced once he was inside and he realized it was not much different from a state prison.

Edwards soon conned two of his fellow inmates into gambling money they couldn't afford to lose; to work off their debt, they provided him with additional money for the commissary each month. With each passing day, the inmate reflected on his time behind bars, but he didn't repent or reform. Instead, Edwards said he decided that after he finished his sentence he would just stick to well-planned federal crimes like forgery, burglary, or armed robbery. If nothing else, living conditions were a little better in federal facilities if he did get caught. However, he doubted he would; he was, after all, an excellent con man, and he was determined that "the world must be made to realize how smart" he was.

If nothing else, Edwards soon proved to be a man of his word. After his release, he focused on burglarizing homes and businesses in the Akron area. In April 1955, he had just been arraigned for the March 9 burglary charge of the Coburn Street home of Glenville Potts. As he left the courtroom, Edwards shoved aside the jailer, Ray Pope, and dashed out of the building. Turning north on High Street, he disappeared into the nearby Palace Theater Arcade. Close to a year passed before authorities caught up to Edwards in Billings, Montana, after he and eighteen-year-old James Melton were arrested there for a string of gas station robberies. He was sentenced to ten years at Montana State Penitentiary in Deer Lodge, Montana. The "monster dungeon," as Edwards called the prison, was situated next door to a brothel in the heart of town and filled with the dregs of society on both sides of the bars. He claimed that many of the guards were transients who were happy to accept bribes to smuggle letters and food into the prisoners; the right amount could also help an inmate avoid harsh conditions and solitary confinement in "the hole."

About a year after Edwards arrived at Deer Lodge, a riot focused statewide attention on the prison, resulting in the firing of the warden and assistant warden. The prisoners were provided with better food and living conditions, as well as a library and the chance to write more than one letter a week. For Edwards, the next two years passed fairly quietly, until his wife Jeanette arrived for a visit one day and announced she was leaving him.

For the first time in his life, Edwards was ready to commit murder. Angered by her desertion, he decided to escape to take his revenge. After two attempts were discovered by the guards, he was forced to serve another two years before he was released on parole. But he was in for another surprise. In July 1959, he was escorted to Portland, Oregon, to stand trial for two armed robberies he had allegedly committed there in 1956. When a local cabinetmaker offered Edwards a job, however, the judge reduced the charges against him to unarmed robbery and sentenced him to five years probation.

Edwards claimed that he did try to change, but the straight life just wasn't for him. He was still bitter about being deserted by his wife, who had obtained a divorce and remarried soon after she left him. He violated his parole to go in search of her, but he soon realized that killing her would only mean going back to jail and he had enough unpleasant memories of his time at Deer Lodge.

Edwards quickly returned to Portland and got a job as a vacuum cleaner salesman, but he noted, "I couldn't handle this respectable success." He was soon spending money even faster than he made it—he bought a new car, a boat, and went out to nightclubs every week. Before long, he acquired a new wife, who actually believed that his dates with other women were part of his cover for the secret anti-communist work he claimed to be performing on behalf of the government.

With at least a half dozen women on a string, Edwards needed more cash. He met a shady lawyer at a bar one night who persuaded him to try his skill at a new scheme—faking automobile accidents. The ex-con managed to collect almost $20,000 in insurance settlements before the authorities came after him. Arrested for fraud, Edwards once again escaped from custody by having a friend pose as a bail bondsman. He continued to elude authorities until 1960, when he was arrested for robbery in Portland, Oregon. But Edwards remained unconcerned, and on December 10 of that year, he broke out of jail again, a feat that quickly earned him a place on the FBI's list of ten most wanted fugitives.

While taking the train south from New York one day with his latest wife in tow, Edwards noticed that a fellow passenger was reading an article about him in the latest edition of *True Detective* magazine. The article, which he included in his biography, noted that Edwards was wanted by federal authorities for unlawful flight after escaping from jail but his "fondness for tattoos" would make him easy to spot. In addition to bearing his own name on his upper right arm, Edwards wore the name "Jeanette," as well as the words "Devil Dog," and "U.S.M.C." According to the article, the FBI considered him a "go-for-broke" fugitive, one who would shoot it out with authorities rather than return to jail.

While another man might have kept a low profile in order to avoid arrest, Edwards decided to start 1962 by robbing a branch of the First National Bank in Akron of more than $7,000. According to an article by Patricia Simms in the August 11, 2009, edition of *Wisconsin State Journal*, "In January 1962, detectives broke down the door of Ed Edwards's two-room rental in Atlanta, scooping up one of the FBI's 10 Most Wanted Fugitives and his 19-year-old wife, Marlene, without a fight." Edwards allegedly still had most of the money from the robbery, even after buying himself a 1958 Cadillac.

Later that year, he was sentenced to Leavenworth Federal Penitentiary in Leavenworth, Kansas, which at that time was the largest maximum security prison in the United States. Sentenced to fifteen years for bank robbery and unlawful flight for his earlier jailbreaks, the twenty-eight-year-old entered the prison as he always had in the past—rebellious, arrogant, and resentful. But for the first time, Edwards found himself experiencing a change of heart regarding his life, thanks primarily to a prison guard named John Alexander.

Providing support and encouragement, Alexander persuaded the younger man to pursue a high school equivalency degree and to start thinking seriously about a trade. In his autobiography, Edwards stated, "As my energy became redirected into positive channels, my bitterness and sarcasm waned to almost the vanishing point." Before long, he soon had another outlet for his energy. In the late 1960s, the law changed to allow inmates the chance to take college classes. Edwards saw it as an opportunity to prove wrong all the people who claimed he was of limited intelligence. He began college courses while at Leavenworth and continued to attend classes after he was transferred to a medium-security prison in Lewisburg, Kansas. There, he received an associate of arts degree from Highland Junior College in 1967 and also made a new friend, the notorious labor leader James Hoffa.

After Hoffa arrived at the prison, Edwards said, "Jimmy and I had become friends almost instantly." He claimed that Hoffa offered to help him find work after he was released from Lewisburg, which would greatly increase his chance of parole. A short time later, a telegram arrived from the Teamsters Union in Akron, promising him a job, and not long afterward, his long-awaited parole was granted.

After leaving jail, Edwards said he was still influenced by Alexander, who had encouraged him to write his autobiography, which was published in 1972 by Hart Publishing Company of New York. For a time after his release, Edwards seemed genuinely interested in changing his ways. He toured and lectured about his personal transformation and also spoke to different groups and organizations about security precautions and safety issues. In addition, he claimed to have worked as a distributor for Sentry-Sonic burglar alarms. The media reported that an Akron film producer bought the movie rights to Edwards's book, two years after it was published, but no film was ever made.

After his autobiography was released, Edwards left Akron for Florida, but by the summer of 1980, he and his family were in Wisconsin living near the Concord House, just east of Johnson Creek. Then, by December 1982, the allegedly reformed criminal was back in jail in Pennsylvania after being convicted of arson for burning down the house he had been renting. About ten years later, the Edwards family had reportedly moved to Cleveland, but around 2000, they relocated to Louisville, Kentucky.

When someone is arrested following a cold case investigation, other police departments sometimes review their files to see if that person might be a possible suspect in any of their unsolved cases. As of this writing, Akron police were investigating to see if Edwards was involved in the 1979 murders of seventeen-year-old Mary Leonard and nineteen-year-old Ricky Beard. The teens disappeared while on a date and their bodies were not discovered until 1985.

Authorities also reexamined the case of Dannie Boy Edwards, a young drifter who moved in with the Edwards family in 1994 and went missing two years later. Edwards was questioned at the time about the young man's disappearance, but no evidence was produced to link him to the body, which was found by a hunter in a shallow grave just behind Troy Cemetery on U.S. Route 422 in Geaugua County—less than a mile from the home Dannie had shared with the Edwards family. Although christened Dannie Law Gloeckner, he had legally changed his name to Edwards after living with the family for more than a year. The Edwards family left their rented home on Claridon Troy Road and moved to Arizona soon after the boy's body was found.

In February 2010, the *Daily Union* of Fort Atkinson, Wisconsin, reported that Jefferson County Circuit Court judge William Hue had ruled that Edwards's case would be heard before a jury selected from that county. Unable to attend the hearing because of his poor health, the accused watched the proceedings by video connection from the Dodge Correctional Institution in Waupun, Wisconsin, where he was receiving medical treatment. During the hearing, public defender Jeffrey De La Rosa withdrew his previous motion for a change of venue. According to the judge, a panel of Jefferson County residents would be able to make an impartial decision in the thirty-year-old murder case. Counsel for the defense, however, did cite the extensive publicity his client had received since his arrest the preceding year. According to the newspaper account, he deemed the coverage, which described Edwards's earlier life as a bank robber and fugitive, as prejudicial to his client. WMTV 15, a television station in Madison, Wisconsin, regularly featured stories about the Hack-Drew murders, and someone who saw one of the reports then contacted police about Edwards.

A jury would not get the opportunity to decide Edwards's guilt in the Hack–Drew murders: Edwards pleaded guilty to the crimes in June 2010 and was sentenced to two consecutive life terms. But the killer will not be doing his prison time in Wisconsin; he is currently serving consecutive life terms in Ohio for the 1977 murders of Billy Lovaco and Judy Straub. Edwards pleaded guilty to those slayings in June 2010, just weeks before entering his plea in the Wisconsin case. Edwards also confessed in a June 2010 interview to the murder of Dannie Boy Edwards. As of this writing, charges had yet to be filed in that case.

America was a divided country in the 1960s and '70s, as more soldiers were sent to the southeast Asian country of Vietnam. While some supported the fight against the spread of communism, others felt that the United States had no business trying to police other countries. Anti-war protesters regularly took to the streets, often sparking a violent response, but most Americans were stunned on May 4, 1970, when four college students were killed and nine others wounded during an antiwar demonstration on the campus of Kent State University in the small city of Kent.

About 2,000 students had participated in the demonstration, which was decried by Gov. James Rhodes as un-American. He called in the Ohio National Guard to disperse the crowd, but when the students refused to leave, the soldiers approached them with bayonets fixed to their rifles. Without warning, the guardsmen suddenly opened fire. When the shooting stopped, two of the protesters, Allison Krause and Jeffrey Miller, were dead, along with two other students, Sandra Scheuer and William Schroeder, who were simply walking across campus to get to their next classes.

In the weeks that followed, about four million outraged students across the country participated in strikes to protest what they saw as a crime. They were often confronted by conservatives who believed with equal conviction that America had a responsibility to fight in Vietnam. The incident at Kent State provoked nationwide debate on whether the shootings of American citizens were legally justified. That June, President Richard Nixon established the President's Commission on Campus Unrest, known as the Scranton Commission, which found no justification for the guardsmen's use of deadly force. But while eight of the guardsmen were indicted by a grand jury, they were ultimately exonerated for their part in what later became known as the Kent State massacre.

CHAPTER 6
Betraying the Mob

Although the Ohio mob may not have been as large as some others, its members fought fiercely over the years to maintain control of their diverse criminal enterprises, including gambling, labor racketeering, and drugs. But what could they do when one of their own bosses decided to turn government informant?

Most people think of New York or New Jersey when they hear the words "Mafia" or *La Cosa Nostra*, because many Italian immigrants settled in those states in the late nineteenth and early twentieth centuries, But the criminal syndicate, rooted in Sicily and southern Italy since the early 1800s, quickly moved westward with honest Italians who migrated to America and moved to Ohio in search of new opportunities. Most of the newcomers who arrived in the Buckeye State worked hard to achieve the American dream, but there was a handful among them who decided that they preferred to extort rather than earn their living. They banded together, and like their brethren on the East Coast, the members of the Ohio mob soon extended their activities to include gambling, prostitution, and any other profitable venture they could find, whether legal or illegal.

A branch of *La Familia* soon flourished in Cleveland, a wide-open town with a reputation for a corrupt city government and police officers who, for the right price, looked the other way. The advent of Prohibition proved to be especially profitable for the Cleveland mob, because it was easy to smuggle alcohol into the state over the border from Canada by way of Lake Erie. In addition, fortunes were made by men who supplied sugar and other raw materials for homemade alcohol. Competition for business soon turned fierce and bloody as the members of rival mobs murdered each other in the streets.

For generations, the fortunes of the Cleveland mob continued to rise as it expanded its business interests—both legal and illegal—throughout the state into the surrounding regions. But in 1983, even hardened Mafiosi and veteran law enforcement officers were shocked when seventy-two-year-old Angelo Lonardo, the former boss of the Cleveland Mafia, turned government informant. Lonardo wasn't the first Mafioso to ever talk to the feds, but he was the son of a mobster and had been one himself for his entire adult life, first as a soldier, then an underboss, and finally as a boss.

What motivated Lonardo to break the *omerta*, the mob's traditional "code of silence," by which he had lived for so long? He had only served as boss of the Cleveland Mafia for about a year when he was arrested and convicted on multiple counts of drug trafficking and racketeering charges. Sentenced that January to a life term plus one hundred and three years at Lewisburg Federal Penitentiary in Pennsylvania, Lonardo, in poor health, had apparently decided he would rather make a deal with the authorities than spend the rest of his life in jail. He contacted the FBI after his first judicial appeal was denied and offered to tell them what he knew, not just about the Cleveland mob but Mafia activities throughout the United States.

In response, the FBI removed Lonardo from prison and began recording his testimony. At that time, the former don was considered to be the highest-ranking mobster to ever inform against the Mafia. Thanks to his testimony, along with that of Jimmy Fratianno of the Los Angeles family, federal prosecutors were ultimately able to convict New York mob bosses Anthony Salerno of the Genovese family, Anthony Corallo of the Luchesse clan, and Carmine Persico of the Colombo family.

Most people were surprised by Lonardo's decision to testify because his family had been one of the first to join the Cleveland Mafia, which at that time was still a loose fraternity of gangs. The four Lonardo brothers arrived in Ohio in the early twentieth century, moving to America from their home in Licata, Sicily, with their good friends and fellow sulphur miners, the seven Porello brothers. Rather than wielding a pick and shovel anymore, Lonardo's father, Joe, became a *capo*, or boss, of a gang that soon dominated criminal activity in Cleveland. With the advent of Prohibition, Joe amassed a personal fortune selling sugar to bootleggers. Apparently, his activities were supported by the Genovese family in New York, which represented the Cleveland mob on the Commission, a board that supervised Mafia activities throughout the United States. When he testified on April 4, 1988, before the Permanent Subcommittee on Investigations of the Committee on Governmental Affairs, Lonardo confirmed the following: "Since the 1920s, my family has reported to the Genovese family in New York City. We always had a very good relationship with the Genovese family, and that is why they represent us on the Commission."

The Lonardo family's business and personal fortunes, however, suffered after Joe went to visit family in Sicily, leaving his brother John in charge. John, who didn't have his brother's head for business, was soon losing about $5,000 a week to the competition, which, ironically, had been established in 1926 by Joe Porello, one of his brother's former lieutenants. According to www.americanmafia.com, "Porello and his six brothers pooled their money and eventually became successful corn sugar dealers headquartered in the upper Woodland Avenue area around East 110th Street." When Joe returned from Sicily six months later, he and John arranged to meet with the Porellos at their barbershop, but on October 13, 1927, the two men were shot and killed after they walked into an ambush at the rear of the store.

Although the Porellos were arrested for the murders, the charges were later dropped for lack of evidence. Joe Porello soon succeeded Joe Lonardo as the sugar distributor for regional bootleggers and later assumed the role of boss of the Cleveland Mafia. Angered by this apparent disrespect toward his father and the loss of their family fortune, eighteen-year-old Lonardo and his cousin, Dominic Sospirato, sought revenge. On June 11, 1929, Lonardo's mother, Carmeline, drove them to a cigar store at the corner of East 110th and Woodland that was owned by the Porellos, where they shot and killed "Black Sam" Todaro, a Porello confederate.

THE CLEVELAND MOB BOSSES

Following the reign of Joseph Lonardo (1919–27), the Cleveland branch of the Mafia was led by Joseph Porello (1927–30), who was in turn succeeded by Frank Milano (1930–35) of the Mayfield Road Mob. In the years that followed, some bosses ruled briefly, like Joseph Romano, who stepped in for a year before he was killed by Angelo Lonardo. In 1936, Alfred Polizzi took over for the next nine years and his successor, John Scalish, remained as capo from 1946 to 1976. After Scalish died, he was followed by Jack Licavoli (1976–85), with Angelo Lonardo named as interim boss in 1981. Lonardo was succeeded by John Tronolone (1985–91), and Anthony Liberatore (1991–93). Although Joseph Iacobacci was said to have retired in 2006, after a thirteen-year reign, many believe that he still retained his authority as boss. Today, the Cleveland Mafia is believed to be run by Russell Papalardo.

Todaro had formerly worked for the Lonardos, and they believed he was partially responsible for killing Lonardo's father and uncle. When Carmeline was questioned, she told police she had stayed in the car and had no idea what had happened inside the store. While few other witnesses appeared at the trial to recount what happened that day, according to www.americanmafia.com, "For the first time in Cleveland's bootleg murder history, justice was served as both young men were convicted and sentenced to life."

Both Lonardo and his cousin, however, were freed after serving a year and a half in jail, after they were given new trials. Acquitted in December 1931, Lonardo soon became a respected member of Frank Milano's Mayfield Road Mob, which included other former members of the Lonardo gang. Milano's crew, rivals of the Porello family, soon joined forces with the Chicago Syndicate headed by Moe Dalitz, a confederate of legendary mobster Meyer Lansky, who had helped Charles "Lucky" Luciano organize mob activities in the United States. The Syndicate was not only responsible for importing alcohol from Canada, but was among the first to see the potential of building gambling casinos in Las Vegas.

In the meantime, Lonardo apparently was not finished seeking retribution against the Porellos. On February 28, 1932, the Cleveland *Plain Dealer* reported that the twenty-one-year-old, who then lived at 13700 Larchmere Boulevard in Shaker Heights, had been locked up the night before at the Central Police Station for questioning in connection with the murders of Raymond and Rosario Porello and one of their henchmen, Dominic Gueli. Arrested at his home by detectives Edward Kartisek and Francis McNamara, Lonardo denied any knowledge of the murders. While the Porellos and Gueli were shot in a cigar store at 11103 Woodland Avenue, the police once again had difficulty in rounding up any witnesses, even among those hurt in the shooting. The newspaper stated, "Frank Brancato, who staggered into St. John's Hospital a few hours after the murders with a bullet wound in his abdomen, was still in a serious condition last night. He either would not or could not talk to police."

After Prohibition was repealed in 1933, the Cleveland mobsters fought one another fiercely as they tried to expand their business ventures. They used guns, knives, baseball bats, and on occasion even ratted out one another to the authorities. In June 1939, Lonardo was one of nine mobsters indicted on charges of running a numbers racket. He was sleeping in an apartment at 3122 Beckett Road in Shaker Heights when the police arrived. Lonardo and his cousin, Angelo Scerria, were arrested by Lieutenant Alfred Jones and transported to police headquarters. According to the Cleveland *Plain Dealer*, Lonardo, "dressed in a smart green summer suit and wearing brown and white shoes, was placed in a fourth-floor cell block with eight others under indictment in the racket who have been unable to post bond." But before long, he was released and returned to the family business, where his record soon earned him a promotion as a "made man" into the Cleveland Mafia.

The following is part of Lonardo's testimony before the federal commission:

> During the '30s, the Commission put a "freeze" on the making of new members . . . since families, especially in New York, were not making the "right" kind of people. Some individuals were even buying their way into the LCN. I have heard that one businessman paid $50,000 to join the LCN. Because of the decree, I was not made into the Cleveland family until the 1940s.
>
> When I was "made" or became a member of La Cosa Nostra, I went through an initiation ceremony. I later learned that to be proposed for membership in La Cosa Nostra, you would have to have killed someone and stood up to the pressure of police scrutiny. Today, you do not have to kill to be a member, but just prove yourself worthy by keeping your mouth shut or by being a "stand-up" guy. However, if you are called upon to kill someone, you have to be prepared to do it.

Lonardo told the commission that he had been proposed for membership in the family because he had avenged his father's murder in 1932. He also acknowledged that in 1933 he and his cousin, John Demarco, murdered Dr. Joseph Romano, a former boss of the Cleveland mob, because he believed Romano had played a part in the death of his father:

> At the time, I was not a member of the LCN, but Demarco was. As a result of the Romano murder, Demarco was condemned to death by the Commission for killing a boss without okaying it with the commission. I was excused for my part in the murder, since I was not an LCN member and did not know the rules.

Lonardo told federal authorities that he later went to Miami with Al Polizzi, who was then the boss of the Cleveland mob. There, Polizzi defended DeMarco's actions before other Commission members and managed to get the death sentence lifted.

By the late 1940s, Polizzi was tired of the ongoing mob wars and the Midwestern winters, so he retired to Florida. Around 1949, John Scalish took over as boss of the Cleveland family, which numbered between fifty and sixty members at that time. According to Lonardo, Scalish did not want to make any new members at that time, so the size and strength of the organization was reduced as older members retired or died. But even though the Cleveland family wasn't that large, it was respected enough to maintain a profitable affiliation with the Chicago Syndicate.

In the late 1940s, mob money from Cleveland was used to finance construction of the Desert Inn casino in Las Vegas, Nevada, as Lonardo recalled:

> A few years after the Desert Inn was licensed and operating, [the owners] gave Al Polizzi, John King, and Frank Milano a piece of the Desert Inn in exchange for the Cleveland family's protection. During the 1970s, the Cleveland family received money from two

sources. The first source was the "skim" money from the Las Vegas casinos, and the second was our piece of the Pittsburgh family's Youngstown, Ohio, rackets.

Our family received about $40,000 a month from Vegas and twenty-five percent of the Youngstown rackets, which would average about $5,000 per month. I did not learn about this arrangement until I became the underboss in 1976. The skim of the Las Vegas casinos started in the early 1970s. Starting in 1974, 1 began receiving about $1,000 to $1,500 a month from the family. I did not know where the money was coming from, but I suspected that it was from the Las Vegas casinos.

Under Scalish, Lonardo rapidly moved up in the ranks of the sixty-member organization. He was an obedient soldier who accepted all assignments, including collecting pay-offs from the casino industry that was also growing in western Pennsylvania and Kentucky. In addition to collecting from the Desert Inn, the Cleveland Mafia received a monthly tribute for their protection from the owners of the Beverly Hills Supper Club, a casino in Covington, Kentucky, Lenardo said. This profitable system remained in place through the 1970s, when Lonardo was named underboss of the Cleveland mob.

There was a brief power vacuum after Scalish died of natural causes in 1976. Although Lonardo was expected to step into his position, Jack Licavoli was named the new boss soon afterward. Lonardo's testimony continued:

At first, Licavoli did not want the job, but I told him to take it, as those were Scalish's wishes. Later, Licavoli made Leo Moceri his underboss and Tony DelSanter his consigliere. One day, I asked Licavoli if he had gone to New York and introduced himself to Tony Salerno as boss of the family. Licavoli said no, and that he did not know that he had to do this. I told him that it was only right, out of respect, since the Genovese family represents us, Cleveland, on the

Commission. After this conversation, Licavoli went to New York to introduce himself as boss of our family.

Unfortunately, Licavoli's ascension drew attention not only from competitors outside of the family, but also from members of the Cleveland mob who were ready to challenge him for control. Another family member named John Nardi, who had little respect for the don, ordered Moceri to be murdered to undermine Licavoli's position. Nardi, who was involved in labor racketeering, apparently felt that the new boss was not a strong enough leader to hold the family together. His attitude created a lot of internal dissension with other members of the Cleveland mob.

Nardi's feud with the family escalated further after he became more closely associated with an Irish gangster named Danny Greene, whom he had hired to kill Moceri. A violent war erupted between the Cleveland Mafia and Greene, who with Nardi's support had attempted to usurp the mob's control of the union rackets. Cleveland residents who were old enough to remember the street wars of Prohibition probably felt as though they had stepped back in time when almost forty car bombs exploded throughout the city in the years that followed. Lonardo recounted the following:

In 1976, after the murder of Moceri, Licavoli and I went to New York to talk to Salerno to obtain his help in murdering Danny Greene and John Nardi. Nardi and Greene had taken a trip to New York to see Paul Castellano about a meat business. Salerno agreed to speak to Castellano and to have Nardi and Greene murdered on their next trip to New York. Nardi and Greene never made a second trip to New York, so New York never helped in their murders.

Adored by the Irish community and despised by the Cleveland Mafia who viewed him as dangerous competition, Greene was as determined to wipe out his business rivals as they were to kill him. Although Nardi was killed by a car bomb in May 1977, eight efforts to eliminate Greene failed completely. The Irishman mocked the mobsters after each failed attempt and Cleveland's reputation began to suffer with other Mafia families. Finally, they decided to hire Ray Ferritto who, with Ronald Carabbia, successfully detonated a bomb in Greene's car when he left his dentist's office. But after Greene was killed, Ferritto turned state's witness when he learned that the Cleveland crime family allegedly wanted him dead. His testimony helped authorities convict many mobsters, including Licavoli, who was sent to prison in 1982 for Greene's murder.

When Licavoli was convicted, Lonardo took control of the Cleveland mob, but arrests on drug trafficking and other criminal charges, as well as internal dissension, had successfully reduced the impact of their branch of the Mafia. With the family in shambles, the new boss's efforts to regroup were halted that same year when he was implicated in a cocaine operation being run by Joey Gallo, one of his lieutenants. Gallo apparently was ambitious and hoped to gain the support of other young mob members by generating a new source of income for the family.

Although Lonardo denied his involvement, he soon found himself behind bars. He later testified before the federal commission:

> Greed is causing younger members to go into narcotics without the knowledge of the families. These younger members lack the discipline and respect that made "This Thing" as strong as it once was. However, this does not mean that La Cosa Nostra is finished in Cleveland or elsewhere.

After he turned on his Mafia connections, the former don was hustled into the federal witness protection program, where he remained for many years before returning to Cleveland. He died at home on April 1, 2006, at age ninety-five, and was buried in Calvary Cemetery in his hometown.

Meanwhile, Cleveland was not the only city in Ohio to become home to the Mafia. About fifty miles south of the lakefront city,

Canton became the base of operations for Pasquale Ferruccio by the 1930s. Born in Canton around 1917, Ferruccio confessed in 1991 to federal authorities that he was part of the gambling rackets that extended through Ohio, Kentucky, and Pennsylvania between 1978 and 1988. He used the Liberty Vending Company, a business that he had founded in his hometown, as a front for his illegal activities.

Following a plea bargain, Ferruccio was sentenced to thirty months in jail and a $100,000 fine. In exchange, prosecutors dropped other charges against him, including and operating an illegal gambling business and interstate travel on behalf of such a business. The indictment of Ferruccio was the conclusion of a three-year investigation by the Internal Revenue Service and the FBI, according to the Cleveland *Plain Dealer*. Ferruccio was one of the mobsters who was turned in by Lonardo, who had done business with him in the past. Lonardo testified that Ferruccio was a "made" member of the LaRocca Family of Pittsburgh, and had served as a liaison between the two mob families.

Ferruccio went back to prison a short time after serving twenty-seven months of his sentence. This time, he was charged with violating his probation by meeting with Lennie Strollo, who was also reportedly affiliated with the Pittsburgh Mafia. Sentenced to two years in jail, Ferruccio had an additional year added to his sentence when he was indicted by a federal grand jury in Pittsburgh for trying to conceal his ownership of gambling operations at the Rincon Indian Reservation Casino near San Diego. Ferruccio and Dominic Strollo, Lennie's brother, apparently had bribed an Indian tribal council member in California to approve a contract that allowed them to run a casino on the reservation. As a convicted criminal, Ferruccio was not permitted to be involved in any phase of casino operations; however, he also reportedly shared ownership of a hotel and gambling casino in Puerto Rico with Lennie Strollo. Ferruccio died in 2005, a month before his eighty-ninth birthday.

By the end of Prohibition, Toledo's mob was run by Thomas Licavoli, who opened his own distilleries and gambling casinos soon after he arrived there. Before long, he expanded his operations throughout northern Ohio, often going to war with other mobsters over lucrative businesses. In March 1934, Licavoli was indicted along with twelve other Mafiosi for the murder of a Toledo bootlegger named Jackie Kennedy. Although sentenced to life in the Ohio State Penitentiary, Licavoli still ran his business from behind bars. He was given special treatment by prison officials and also allowed visits from other prominent mobsters, like Michael D'Angelo of Columbus. Both Preston Thomas and his successor, James Woodard, were fired from their posts as wardens for their treatment of Licavoli, who had also organized a thriving gambling and narcotics business within the prison.

Although the mobster's influence apparently was far-reaching, no one expected it to extend to the governor's office. Many people were surprised when Gov. James Rhodes announced in January 1969 that he had commuted Licavoli's sentence from first to second degree murder. Despite public outrage, Rhodes refused to change his decision, which meant that Licavoli would be eligible almost immediately for parole. Released in 1971, the well-known mob figure died of cancer two years later and was buried in Mount Cisco Cemetery in Detroit.

Rhodes apparently was not the only Ohio politician to have fallen under the Mafia's influence. Youngstown was known as "Murder City, U.S.A." because of all of the bodies that the mob allegedly has dumped into the Meander Reservoir. Built in 1929 on the Meander Creek, the reservoir was designed to provide fresh water to surrounding communities. The mob literally got away with murder in Youngstown for many years, because it allegedly controlled both local politicians and the Youngstown police force. In 1980, the city was the site of a mob war between the Carabbia brothers, who were loyal to the Cleveland family, and a gang led by Joey Naples and James Prato, who reported to Pittsburgh. But for the first time, both factions were confronted by a new opponent, James Traficant, the newly-appointed Sheriff of Mahonig County.

Traficant, who had run on the Democratic ticket, declared himself the mob's worst nightmare and offered the voters a strong anti-drug platform. He won the election by a landslide, but what he didn't tell the voters was that the Carabbias had offered to fund his campaign—an offer that Traficant claimed he soundly rejected. He assumed his post on January 5, 1981, but in August 1982, the new sheriff was indicted by a federal grand jury for accepting bribes from organized crime. Traficant refused an offer of immunity from prosecution if he resigned his post as sheriff and his trial began in Cleveland in May 1983.

Witnesses for the prosecution swore that James Prato, the underboss of the Youngstown Mafia, and other mob members had donated more than $160,000 in cash to Traficant when he was campaigning for sheriff. In exchange, the new sheriff was supposed to ignore their illegal gambling operations. Traficant, acting as his own attorney, told the court that he had returned the money. Although the prosecution had a mountain of evidence, the defendant managed to persuade a jury of his innocence. On June 15 of that year, after four days of deliberation, the panel returned a verdict of not guilty.

The public support Traficant received during the trial persuaded him to run for Congress. In 1984, he defeated six other Democratic candidates in the primary and later beat Lyle Williams, the Republican candidate, by almost 20,000 votes. Unfortunately, his transition to Washington apparently did not cause him to change his ways. Two years later, Traficant appeared in the U.S. Tax Court, where he was found liable for taxes on bribes received from the mob. Cleared at that time of any criminal charges related to the bribes, he was reelected to office eight more times. But the courts weren't through with him yet.

The media reported that the FBI had observed Strollo and other reputed organized crime figures meeting with Charles O'Nesti, director of Traficant's district office, at a restaurant in Boardman in November 1996. A spokesman for Traficant later denied that any meeting had taken place, but in 2002, Traficant was convicted of bribery and racketeering charges and spent the next seven years behind bars. Prosecutors and witnesses said he filed false tax returns and accepted free labor and materials for his Ohio farm from contractors in exchange for giving them congressional favors. Even though he was the only the second House member since the Civil War to be voted out for unethical behavior, about one thousand people in Youngstown reportedly turned out for a "welcome home" dinner after he returned to his hometown.

The congressman had also been tied to Lennie Strollo, who was believed to be the head of organized crime activity in the Mahoning Valley since 1991 after Joey Naples was fatally wounded at the site of a home he was building in Beaver Township, near Youngstown. According to the Cleveland *Plain Dealer*, while Strollo and Naples had maintained their own factions that controlled different areas of Mahoning County, the FBI believed that the two men had shared control of illegal gambling in the Youngstown area after James Prato retired as boss in the mid-1980s. They allegedly operated casinos, numbers lotteries, and illegal video poker machines. But Strollo apparently did not trust his partner. Convicted of racketeering in 1990 for running an illegal gambling operation that included the All-American Club in Campbell, and for bribing a Mahoning County sheriff's deputy and a local police chief, Strollo reportedly feared that Naples would take over his gambling operations once he went to prison.

The FBI said Strollo controlled area gambling in association with Henry Zottola, described as a high-ranking associate of the Pittsburgh mob, who served as a liaison between the Pittsburgh crime family and the Youngstown Mafia. Strollo was believed to have been involved in the murder of rival mobster Ernie Biondillo Jr., who was killed in June 1996. An informant told FBI agent John Stoll that two men had been offered a $35,000 contract to get rid of Biondillo because Strollo believed the other man was trying to take over some of his empire.

Biondillo, who owned a vending company, reportedly was bribing local politicians without telling Strollo, and placing his video poker games in private clubs in Hillville, Pennsylvania, a region that Strollo controlled. Strollo demanded that Biondillo either remove the machines or share the profits, but when he refused to cooperate, Strollo reportedly ordered him to be killed. Two Youngstown men were later charged in Biondillo's murder. Cleveland Blair, twenty-five, and George Wilkins, twenty-four, pleaded guilty to a federal charge of committing murder to further a racketeering enterprise. Wilkins, who had attempted to pawn a diamond ring belonging to Biondillo at a Pittsburgh jewelry store, was also later charged with the attempted murder of newly elected Mahoning County prosecutor Paul Gains in December 1996.

According to federal authorities, the mob has been involved in a variety of activities in Youngstown, including robbery, burglary, gambling, bribery, and extortion, as well as drug trafficking and murder for hire. Arrested by the FBI in 1997 during a crackdown on organized crime, Strollo later turned state's witness in exchange for twelve years in a federal prison. In addition to testifying against former congressman James Traficant, former Mahoning County judge Martin W. Emrich, and former Youngstown municipal judge Andrew Polovischak Jr., Strollo provided information about a number of unsolved homicides and mob activities in Cleveland, Pittsburgh, Detroit, and New York. With credit for time already served and for good behavior, he was released in 2004. Since he had previously transferred all of his assets into his wife's hands, Strollo reportedly returned to living a very comfortable lifestyle after he was released from prison.

Donald Harvey was one of the "quiet types" who was never suspected of any crime, let alone murder. But in 2010, the polite young man who was born in Butler County in 1952 was known as inmate number A-199449 and was serving four consecutive life terms at the Southern Ohio Correctional Facility in Lucasville. Harvey, then fifty-eight, was believed to be responsible for killing at least one dozen terminally ill patients while working as an orderly in Marymount Hospital in London, Kentucky. His crimes, some of which were also committed at Cincinnati's V.A. Medical Hospital and Drake Memorial Hospital, remained undetected for almost twenty years. While it is unlikely that anyone will ever know the number of people he really killed, current figures range from thirty-six to eighty-seven.

Harvey, who also worked as a nursing assistant, a housekeeping aide, a cardiac-catheterization technician, and an autopsy assistant at the different hospitals, considered himself an "Angel of Death," who only killed to ease the suffering of those patients who had little hope of recovery. He used a variety of drugs, including arsenic and cyanide, but also suffocated some of his victims. During the investigation, authorities learned that their suspect was a self-professed occultist who "practiced" poisoning family members and friends, whom he would then nurse back to health.

Harvey confessed to the hospital killings, but initially pleaded not guilty by reason of insanity. In August 1987, however, he pleaded guilty in Cincinnati to twenty-four counts of aggravated murder, four counts of attempted murder, and one count of felonious assault. He was sentenced to four consecutive life terms, without the possibility of parole. After being extradited to Kentucky for the killings committed there, Harvey pleaded guilty to nine counts of murder and was sentenced to nine additional life terms. In February 1988, he appeared in court in Cincinnati once again where he entered a plea of guilty for three more homicides and three attempted murders. The court sentenced him to three life terms for the murders, and seven to twenty-five years for each of the attempted murder charges.

A decade after Harvey committed his crimes, Ohio residents would find themselves looking at another unlikely murder suspect. But unlike the self-proclaimed "Angel of Death," this one managed to escape prosecution in the end, and at the time of this writing, remains free.

CHAPTER 7

A Deadly Affair

Many people are familiar with the term "love triangle" and the friction that develops when one person becomes jealous of the relationship between the other two. However, one married Ohio woman didn't rest until she created a much more intricate configuration that ultimately resulted in the death of one of her lovers.

On June 16, 2001, Jeffrey Zack, a big guy with a shock of prematurely white hair, pulled his Ford Explorer into the gas station at BJ's Wholesale Club on Home Avenue in Akron. As he stopped beside a gas pump, the forty-four-year-old entrepreneur from Stow was shot and killed by a person dressed in black, wearing a helmet, who suddenly rode up beside his vehicle on a motorcycle similar to a Kawasaki Ninja, with lime green trim. In minutes, spectators gathered at the scene, including Sheila Steer, an emergency room physician who had been shopping inside BJ's when the shooting occurred. As the shooter escaped, Steer, assisted by three nurses who had stopped for gas, attempted to stabilize Zack as they waited for an ambulance. Unfortunately, he died shortly after being transported to Akron City Hospital.

Since the motorcycle was long gone by the time the police arrived, Akron detectives David Whiddon and Vincent Felber weren't able to discover much at the scene other than a bullet fragment, a grainy security camera video, and a sketchy description of Zack's unknown assailant. Randall Addison, who had stopped for gas that day, only caught a glimpse of the motorcycle as it raced away from the station. Carolyn Hyson, the attendant who picked that moment to step outside of the gas station's cash booth, came face to face with the killer but could offer no further information because the motorcycle rider's helmet had tinted glass. Despite such limited clues, the detectives' investigation would eventually pull the lid off of a convoluted saga of adultery, jealousy, betrayal, and murder that would enthrall not just the residents of Ohio but Americans everywhere.

Akron might be the fifth largest city in Ohio, with a population of more than 217,000 people, but only sixteen murders occurred there in 2003. Founded in 1825 along the Cuyahoga River, it was once an industrial center known as the "Rubber Capital of the World." Although its police department had more experience in dealing with burglary and theft cases, it didn't take long for the detectives to discover that Zack was no choir boy. The product of a broken home, he seemed to have resented both of his parents—his father for deserting the family and his mother for remarrying. He periodically left home as a teenager, first running off to Florida when he was sixteen; two years later, he called home to tell his mother he was living on a kibbutz in Israel. Zack claimed that he enlisted while he was living overseas and that he had served as a paratrooper in the Israeli army, participating in a number of covert missions. After he returned to the United States, he never seemed able to settle in one spot for long, making unsuccessful attempts to become a stockbroker and a headhunter, and later moving on to real estate and the scrap metal business. He regularly bent the rules in his professional life, often making his fair share of enemies along the way.

During their investigation, the police learned that three days before Zack was murdered, someone had left a threatening message on his answering machine. Local media reported that the male caller said, "All right buddy, you've got one more out. So you need to start answering your cell phone, okay?"

But there was a chance that the message wasn't related to business, because it seemed that Zack also liked to bend the rules in his personal life. He had a volatile temper, and the police were not surprised to find that he already had a record for charges that included domestic violence, harassment, and involvement in a prostitution ring. Married in 1986 to Bonnie Boucher, he repeatedly cheated on his wife throughout most of their marriage. He chased women—whether they were married or single—often with a zeal that bordered on obsession. In 1996, he reportedly fondled an underage clerk at the same BJ's where he had stopped for gas the day he was shot. Zack had reportedly even been amused when he was banned from the premises after he continued to harass the young woman. Unfortunately, his most serious extramarital relationship would prove to be the one that turned fatal.

About ten years earlier, Zack had started an affair with Cynthia George, the wife of well-known local businessman Ed George. The George family had operated Tangier, a popular Moroccan-themed nightspot in Akron since 1948. Over the years, the club had featured well-known acts such as the Beach Boys, Tina Turner, and Frankie Valli. Zack, who always seemed to be on the lookout for that one chance to acquire the good things in life, apparently thought Cynthia held the key to everything he wanted. She was beautiful, rich, and willing to share; the fact that she was married to an important local businessman undoubtedly added a little spice to the relationship. What Zack failed to realize was that Cynthia was probably the one person who was even more unscrupulous than he was when it came to getting her own way.

The police soon learned that Cynthia had bankrolled Zack's current business venture, which involved servicing vending machines that he owned throughout the state. When authorities found out that Zack had referred to Cynthia as his "girlfriend" to family members and friends, they began to suspect that Ed George, who was believed to have underworld connections, may have been behind the shooting. These suspicions grew when they received little cooperation from the Georges after they attempted to question Cynthia and her husband about their relationship with the murdered man.

Since the George family was well-known and influential in Akron, interdepartmental politics sometimes prevented the detectives assigned to the case from moving as quickly as they would have liked with the investigation. Still, authorities considered Ed to be a viable suspect, because he reportedly had ties to the local underworld. But if that were true, why had Ed contacted the police in reference to Zack's continuing harassment of his wife? Ironically, the additional delays caused by office politics ultimately allowed investigators to take a closer look at Cynthia instead of Ed.

According to Keith Elliot Greenberg and Vincent Felber, the authors of *Perfect Beauty*, the former Cynthia Mae Rohr grew up as part of a devoutly Catholic working class family in North Canton. The vivacious, petite blonde was one of four children born to Glen, a coal miner, and his wife Helen. Although their one-story bungalow was small, it was always well-maintained.

Cynthia was very popular by the time she reached North Canton High School. Not only did she belong to the Pep Club, but she served as president of the Booster Club and volunteered at a local hospital. In her junior year, Cynthia was voted in as a member of the Homecoming Court. Since there was no money to send her to college after she graduated in 1972, Cynthia decided to get out of Ohio and explore the rest of the United States. She later claimed that she had hitchhiked across the country, all the way to Alaska.

For a time, Cynthia worked for US Airways in Pittsburgh, but six years after graduating from high school, she returned to Ohio.

There, the twenty-five-year-old met Ed George at his club. Although Cynthia was living at the time in a trailer on a farm, where she fed the animals in exchange for rent, she claimed that she also booked musical acts. That was her alleged reason for contacting forty-four-year-old Ed, also a devout Catholic, who was soon dazzled by the young woman's beauty and charm.

A self-professed workaholic, Ed willingly forgot about business when he and Cynthia began dating, and before long, he was paying her bills and buying her expensive gifts. By the time they got engaged, Cynthia was actively involved in running the Tangier. In addition to serving as a hostess, she hired new employees and supervised renovations to the club. After a five-year courtship, the couple had an elaborate wedding in 1984 with five hundred guests in attendance. They then moved into a condominium in Granger Township outside of Akron and were soon expecting their first child. In 1987, they hired Mary Ann Brewer, a nurse, to help Cynthia during a difficult second pregnancy. But even though that child had kept her in bed for most of the nine months, she had four more pregnancies in the five years that followed, each one more physically challenging than the last.

Cynthia seemed to bounce back after the birth of each child, throwing herself into Akron's social world and assisting local charities. The Tangier was doing a thriving business, and Ed George, with a beautiful wife and a growing family, was a happy man. Other nannies were hired to help with the children; while many came and went, Brewer remained with the family for the next thirteen years. In 1992, she moved with the Georges into their dream house on eighteen acres in rural Medina County, about twenty miles outside of Akron. Greenberg and Felber described it as: "a five bedroom, five bathroom French/English mini-mansion, with giant chimneys and a 1,429 square foot, four-car garage."

After they moved in, Cynthia set aside a wing of the house with a private entrance for her personal use and began to withdraw from her family and her charity work. Although her rooms were lavishly decorated, she apparently paid little attention to the rest of the house or her children. While Ed seemed to enjoy being a hands-on father to their brood, she seemed content to leave them in the care of Brewer and the other nannies.

Instead, Cynthia began to seek attention elsewhere. Zack, who had introduced himself to the Georges one night at the Tangier, soon become a regular visitor to Cynthia's wing of the palatial home. The two would hide away for hours from the rest of the family in the attic

CRIME AMONG THE AMISH

The Amish communities throughout the United States are generally recognized for their dedication to old-fashioned virtues, keeping technology to a minimum, and respect for the religion founded by Jakob Ammann in Switzerland in the late seventeenth century. Old Order Amish, who follow the more conservative tenets of their faith, are spread throughout the United States and Canada, but Ohio can lay claim to the largest population, with 55,000 living in the Buckeye State. In recent years, the Amish—like Americans everywhere—have been confronted by an unprecedented level of violence that they never expected to find at their door.

In one incident, a traditional prank resulted in murder charges after a man who threw tomatoes at passing cars in Holmesville was shot and killed by an angry motorist. Authorities reported that after his car was struck several times, Marion Weaver fired rounds from his shotgun into a nearby cornfield where a group of young people had been hiding to throw tomatoes and fire paintball guns at cars. Twenty-three-year-old Steven Keim of Mount Hope, an Amish community about sixty miles south of Cleveland, was killed.

That same month, the residents of Millersburg where shocked by the deaths of an Old Order couple and their adult son, which, according to Holmes County sheriff Timothy Zimmerly, appeared to be a double murder and suicide. Authorities believe that fifty-seven-year-old Mary Edna Mullet and her son Wayne Mullet, twenty-nine, were fatally shot by Mary's or behind a locked bedroom door. Did Ed suspect that the attachment between his wife and their new friend was more than just a casual friendship? If he did, he never did anything to indicate that Zack was not welcome in their home. Cynthia would later claim to be a victim of depression who fell for Zack simply because he was always available while Ed was usually engrossed in business. That same depression, she said, also kept her a prisoner in a relationship that soon turned abusive. Yet, as time passed, she apparently made little effort

husband, fifty-six-year-old Dennis Mullet, who then turned the gun on himself. Mary and Wayne's bodies were discovered in separate bedrooms upstairs in their Salt Creek Township home, while Dennis's body was later found in the basement.

On June 2, 2009, the serenity of rural Wayne County was broken when thirty-year-old Barbara Weaver, a mother of five, was shot to death inside her home. Ten days later, her twenty-nine-year-old husband, Eli, was charged with complicity to commit murder, while Barbara Raber of Millersburg, age thirty-nine, was charged with aggravated murder for firing the fatal shot. The media reported that Eli had reportedly left the house at about 3 A.M. to go on a fishing trip. Though the children were unharmed, Barbara Weaver was discovered dead in her bed about five hours later. Wayne County coroner Amy Jolliff later conducted an autopsy and determined that she had died of a gunshot wound to the chest. Barbara Raber was arrested at home the day after the murder by sheriff's deputies. While Wayne County Sheriff Thomas Maurer declined to speculate about a motive for the murder, he did state that one of the suspects had confessed to the crime.

These are just a few of the crimes that have occurred among the Amish communities in Ohio in recent years. Enforcing the law is sometimes difficult for county and local police departments because the Amish often prefer to punish any crime internally rather than rely on the "English," as outsiders are known. Lawbreakers are often subject to excommunication for a period of time, during which they will be shunned by other members of the community.

to break away. Zack's family, including his wife, knew about the longstanding relationship—and DNA tests later proved that Cynthia's youngest biological child was in fact fathered by her lover.

But murder? It seemed impossible that someone like Cynthia would ever be involved in a fatal shooting. That is, until authorities discovered her connection to John Zaffino.

According to Zaffino's ex-wife, Christine Todaro, he was the person responsible for killing Zack. Hot-tempered and always ready for a fight, Zaffino had previously told her that he had once beaten up a "tall, white-haired Israeli," so she knew he already had reason to dislike the other man. Todaro told authorities that Zaffino had mentioned the murder several times in conversations; while he never admitted to pulling the trigger, he spoke in a way that made her suspicious about his involvement. Todaro had been married to Zaffino between 1999 and 2001 but did not come forward to speak to the police until June 2002. She had good reason: Zaffino had beaten her in the past and she was growing even more afraid for her own safety. After providing the police with enough information for them to investigate further, Todaro agreed to wear a wire to see if Zaffino would say anything more about the murder. When authorities planted a story about the crime in a local newspaper, Todaro called her ex-husband, who warned her against giving his name to the police as a suspect in the case.

Despite her fears, Todaro continued to assist the police in their investigation in the months that followed. Suddenly, new witnesses and evidence surfaced that indicated Zaffino had in fact shot Zack. Two weeks before the murder, Zaffino had purchased two handguns from Bob Cole, a former fellow truck driver at North Canton Transfer. Cole told the police that Zaffino had bought a Davis .32-caliber semiautomatic and a Smith & Wesson .357 with a four-inch barrel from him in March 2001. Authorities knew a .357 had fired the bullet that had killed Zack. They also learned their suspect owned a black Ninja-style motorcycle with lime green stripes that, according to another ex-wife, he had abandoned at her home in Pennsylvania just a few days after the murder. But despite his apparent dislike of Zack, authorities were at a loss to explain why Zaffino would suddenly decide to kill the other man. Enter Cynthia George.

In 2000, Cynthia decided it was time to fulfill several dreams. She became a contestant in the Mrs. Ohio Pageant and finished fourth. And one night she picked up Zaffino at a club called the Groove Shack. Was she planning to use him to help her escape from Zack? Or did she find the volatile thug as attractive as he was dangerous–in many respects just like her other lover? Before long, she was juggling both men as well as the demands of family life. Both Cynthia and Zaffino would later claim that he simply had helped her find the strength to finally end her tumultuous relationship with Zack in May 2001. But she soon began paying Zaffino's bills and buying him expensive gifts, including a cell phone and the motorcycle. Cynthia reportedly discouraged him from going to work so that he would be at her beck and call.

According to authorities, Zaffino was the man on the motorcycle and had killed Zack at Cynthia's bidding, but even after they obtained sufficient evidence to arrest Zaffino for aggravated murder on September 22, 2002, he never implicated Cynthia George. A few days after news of his arrest appeared in the local papers, the case against Zaffino was strengthened from an unexpected source. Detective Whiddon received a telephone call from a ranger at the park by Everett Covered Bridge, who said that Zaffino had been stopped one night and questioned there about a month before the murder. When the ranger saw an empty handgun holster in the car, she became suspicious of his behavior. After the area near Zaffino's vehicle was searched a few days later, the ranger found a loaded gun that matched the description of the one he had purchased from a former coworker. Detectives came to believe that Zaffino had been lying in wait for Zack but was forced to abort his plans when the ranger appeared. They later learned, thanks to a thorough check of her cell phone records, that Cynthia had apparently tried to persuade Zack to meet her at the park that night, where he would have been confronted by Zaffino. But when Zaffino was offered a deal if he would just name Cynthia as the mastermind behind Zack's killing, he refused.

When Zaffino's trial opened in Summit County on February 26, 2003, the sordid details of the case—the illicit affairs, the child fathered by another man, his connection to the socially prominent George family—were secrets confined to an ongoing police investigation. John Zaffino had pleaded not guilty; while prosecutors were convinced that Cindy George was somehow behind the murder plot, they simply didn't have the evidence to charge her. Now, in order for them to convict Zaffino and establish a motive, prosecutors had to reveal Cynthia's secrets to show her ties to both the alleged murderer and the victim. Everything was then exposed to the harsh light of day along with testimony from Zaffino's two ex-wives, providing enough circumstantial evidence for the jury to convict the former truck driver of aggravated murder in March 2003.

Summit County assistant prosecutor Michael Carroll told the court that the accused was acting on behalf of Cynthia George, because Zack had continued to harass her and her husband after their affair ended. Cynthia also feared that her ex-lover would fulfill his threat to take her youngest child—actually his daughter—and move to Israel. Too ashamed to turn to her husband, the only way out for Cynthia, Carroll said, was for someone to kill Zack. When Cynthia was called to testify the following week, she invoked the Fifth Amendment, a right against self-incrimination. Although Zaffino's lawyer argued that the evidence against his client was purely circumstantial, the jury took less than four hours to convict him on March 11. Six days later, he was sentenced to life at the Toledo Correctional Institute, a decision that was later upheld that December by the Ninth District Court of Appeals.

Although the media clamored for further details after Zaffino's trial, the police refused to comment on whether Cynthia would be arrested in connection with the case. Two more years would pass before the authorities were able to gather enough evidence to charge the woman who was considered one of the guiding lights of Akron society. Arrested on January 10, 2005, outside of the Bath & Body Works store in the West Market shopping mall in Bath Township, Cynthia was charged with complicity and conspiracy to commit aggravated murder. Ed, who believed in her innocence, spent $200,000 to bail her out of Summit County Jail.

After repeated postponements, George's five-attorney team opted on November 10 of that same year to have their client appear without a jury before Judge Patricia A. Cosgrove, claiming that all of the publicity had made it impossible for Cynthia to get a fair trial in Summit County.

When the trial opened four days later before the judge, counsel for the defense argued that their client simply had no motive for killing Zack, because she had ended their relationship a month before the murder. It was suggested that Bonnie Zack, tired of enduring her husband's infidelity for so long, was a better suspect that Cynthia. The prosecution, however, claimed there was enough evidence to prove that Cynthia had been the driving force behind Zack's murder even though the case was circumstantial. She persuaded Zaffino to kill Zack to prevent him from exposing their affair and the fact that he had fathered her youngest child. While no weapon had ever been recovered, Zaffino's former co-worker, Robert Cole, testified that he sold Zaffino two handguns, one of which was a .357 magnum, the suspected murder weapon.

When prosecutors brought Zaffino's motorcycle into the courtroom, several witnesses testified that it resembled the one driven by the killer. Zaffino's ex-wife from Pennsylvania testified that its bright lime green stripes had been covered when her former husband dropped the motorcycle at her house. To show Cynthia's connection to the crime, a bank manager testified that the Akron socialite had taken a little less than $5,300 in cash out of the bank on the same day that Zaffino bought the motorcycle. Christine Todaro took the stand once again and related her conversations with Zaffino after Zack was killed. According to the prosecution, the evidence proved that not only had Cynthia encouraged Zaffino to kill her former boyfriend, she had paid for whatever he needed to get the job done.

During the trial, cell phone records showed that Cynthia was on two different phones at the same time on the same night that the ranger questioned Zaffino at the park. On one line, she was talking to Zaffino, while on the other, prosecutors said, she tried to lure Zack there to be ambushed by the other man. When that initial plot fell through, Zaffino decided to kill Zack at the gas station the following month. On that date, Cynthia and Zaffino were talking on their cell phones just a few minutes before Zack was murdered. Twenty minutes later, they were on the telephone once again.

According to the prosecution, Cynthia and Zaffino stayed in touch as he discarded the motorcycle and got rid of any other incriminating evidence. Cell phone records showed that they spoke while Zaffino was on the road back to Ohio after ditching the motorcycle at the home of his unsuspecting first ex-wife. To make sure that her new lover remained loyal, Cynthia continued to shower him with money to pay for his legal defense and made promises, telling him he would run the Tangier for the Georges after he was released from prison.

During the trial, the state was able to show that Cynthia and Ed gave about $15,000 to their lawyers, which was then transferred to Zaffino's attorney to pay his legal fees. Four months later, Zaffino received another $10,000 that was traced to the Georges. The prosecutors also stated that Cynthia promised to make sure that Zaffino's son was financially secure. But the money trail apparently wasn't the only weapon in the prosecution's arsenal. They presented a number of incriminating letters between Cynthia and Zaffino—his containing veiled threats and requests for further assistance and hers filled with pledges of love and support.

In response, the defense declared that Zaffino had taken it upon himself to kill Zack without Cynthia's knowledge. Since Zaffino never implicated George in any of his actions, there simply was not sufficient evidence to convict her of conspiring in the crime. As far as the cell phone calls, Cynthia's lawyers said that no one overheard any conversations that she had been involved in a plot to murder Zack. And the money that had been allegedly paid for Zaffino's legal bills was simply a sharing of expenses, which was a common practice among defense counsel.

When Ed George took the stand as a character witness for his wife, he told the court that he believed his wife was innocent of any involvement in Zack's death. He had believed that Cynthia and her former lover were nothing more than good friends, even when Zack reportedly started making harassing phone calls to her. After more than a week in session, the trial closed on November 23 with the testimony of Ed George, who declared his continuing faith in his wife, and closing summations by the attorneys. The judge announced that she would deliberate over the four-day Thanksgiving holiday and deliver her verdict at 11 A.M. on November 28.

Cynthia went home to enjoy the holiday with her family, optimistic that the verdict would be favorable. But the entire George family was stunned after returning to court. Cosgrove acquitted Cynthia of conspiracy to commit aggravated murder for the earlier attempt on Zack's life at a local park, but found her guilty of complicity to commit aggravated murder for the shooting at the gas station. The vivacious socialite was sentenced to life in prison without the possibility of parole for at least twenty-three years.

As George's attorneys scrambled to prepare an appeal, their client was transported on November 30 to the Ohio Reformatory for Women in Marysville. On December 15, her attorneys filed an appeal with the Ninth District Court of Appeals, which ruled in a two-to-one decision in March 2007 that there was insufficient evidence to convict Cynthia. According to Greenberg and Felber, "The Appeals Court had reached the extremely rare conclusion that the prosecution had not presented any evidence of George's guilt. According to this premise, authorities never even had the right to arrest her in the first place."

The decision, which was upheld that August by the Ohio Supreme Court, effectively allowed Cynthia to go free without fear of ever being tried again for any involvement in Zack's death.

After Cynthia's release, Brian Zack, son of the murdered man, filed a wrongful death lawsuit against Zaffino and the George family that was scheduled to be heard in November 2007. The following October, the Georges appeared before a Summit County probate judge in Akron and agreed on a settlement of $650,000 without admitting any complicity in the case.

Ironically, Detective Vincent Felber wound up facing a ninety-day suspension after coauthoring *Perfect Beauty*, which was critical of the department's work on the Zack murder case. He later chose to accept a seven-day unpaid suspension and forfeit fifteen days of vacation or compensatory time, a settlement that allowed him to return to work in the department's detective bureau.

Local media reported that Cynthia stopped contacting Zaffino after her release. Even though federal prosecutors approached him repeatedly to try and get him to testify against her, Zaffino told the Cleveland *Plain Dealer* that he wasn't going to accuse her because she was not involved in the murder. The police never recovered a murder weapon or any forensic evidence that linked Zaffino or Cynthia to Zack's death. Federal authorities said that Cynthia is still vulnerable to federal charges, however, even though she has been tried and acquitted by the state.

As for Cynthia herself? After her release, she gave several interviews to try and change public opinion of her actions. According to Cynthia, she wasn't spoiled and self-centered but was actually the victim of both physical and mental abuse and mental illness. She claimed that depression led her into an emotional spiral that caused her to compromise her marriage. At first she was infatuated with Zack, but then she grew afraid when he became physically abusive. She claimed that he raped her at her home one night, but she was too ashamed to tell her husband what had happened. In the years that followed, she was simply too afraid of her hot-tempered lover to try and end their affair. But other than Mary Ann Brewer, the George's former nanny, no one witnessed any alleged incidents of violence during the ten years that they were together. Cynthia may have been more afraid that her husband would ask for a divorce, which would have adversely affected both her comfortable social and financial status.

During one interview, Cynthia said she turned to Zaffino, because he was kind to her when they met in 2000. She claimed that without her knowledge or permission, Zaffino killed Zack to try and help her resolve the problem relationship. While Cynthia George remains a free woman today, it is very likely that to many people, she will always be guilty of manipulating John Zaffino to kill her former lover Jeff Zack. It is unlikely that anyone will ever know for certain, because as Greenberg and Felber noted, "To this day, many longtime associates claim that they never really knew her."

Thirty-eight-year-old Rosemarie Essa was on her way to meet a friend when she died on February 24, 2005, after collapsing behind the wheel of her SUV and crashing into another vehicle. Although she was rushed to Hillcrest Hospital, Rosemarie died within the hour. While authorities at first considered her to be the victim of nothing more than a tragic accident, her husband Yazeed Essa was eventually held responsible for her death when the coroner carefully examined her body and found poison in her system.

The coroner had become suspicious when Essa exhibited little grief at his wife's untimely death. In 2010, Essa, a former emergency room physician from Cleveland, was found guilty of aggravated murder after a Cuyahoga County jury convicted him of injecting cyanide into Rosemarie's calcium supplements, which caused her to lose control her vehicle. Although he had disappeared into Lebanon after his wife's death, Essa was extradited in 2009 and returned to Ohio. In 2010, he faced life in prison with the possibility of parole after twenty years.

CHAPTER 8

To Protect and Serve

Looking for a job that offers long hours, just okay pay, and probably the chance to put your life on the line at least once before you retire? Thankfully, the men and women who belong to Ohio's state and municipal police departments have always been willing to do just that.

In the early twentieth century, a rapidly expanding network of highways and roads ran throughout Ohio, allowing both people and products to move more quickly from place to place. To keep those roadways safe, the Ohio state government created a state police force in 1933, after twenty years of debate. It took a while because the idea had previously provoked controversy; union leaders were afraid that a state police force would be called in against workers in the event of a strike. When the legislation was created, it specifically limited the authority of the new Ohio State Highway Patrol

(OSHP) to enforcing motor vehicle laws on roads and banned it from getting involved in strikes or any other type of labor unrest.

According to www.statepatrol.ohio.gov, more than five thousand men between the ages of twenty-four and forty initially applied for sixty openings in the new police force. In addition to six district offices in Toledo, Ravenna, Sidney, Delaware, Cambridge, and Chillicothe, there were three substations in private homes in each district. The first patrolmen drove motorcycles all year long. In its first year, the OSHP created a statewide radio network, which provided law enforcement officials with the ability to communicate throughout the state. The OSHP also made more than four thousand arrests and issued citations to more than 120,000 drivers. These achievements prompted the Ohio state legislature to double the size of the force by 1935, and in 1941 that number was increased to three hundred patrolmen. In 1968, the state government decided that the OSHP should always employ a minimum of 880 officers. By the late twentieth century, the agency played an important role in stopping the flow of illegal drugs, a problem that still exists today, according to Staff Lieutenant Monte Morgan.

"Drugs are a big problem," said Morgan. "I'm stationed at the Ohio Turnpike, which is a major pipeline from the east coast. We constantly see drugs flowing east and cash flowing west."

The veteran officer, who has served twenty-eight years with the Ohio State Highway Patrol, noted that authorities have seen a shift in the types of crime that occur these days in the Buckeye State. He noted, "In addition to drugs, there is more identity theft and home invasions." Although he has been an administrator for the past eight years, Morgan still likes to get out on the road to assist his fellow patrol officers whenever possible. Morgan wasn't planning on a career in law enforcement after he graduated from high school, but a job as a cadet dispatcher for the State Highway Patrol soon changed his mind. In 1984, Morgan underwent twenty-one weeks of training at the Ohio State Highway Patrol Academy in Columbus. There, in addition to the same basic courses provided to municipal police officers, he underwent extra physical training and spent extra time learning traffic law.

Although he wondered at first if he had made the right career choice, Morgan soon adjusted to life at the Akron highway patrol post, which was his first assignment. While riding with an experienced officer for a six-month probation period, he was thrilled to participate in the recovery of two stolen vehicles. At the end of his probation, Morgan was then handed the keys to his own vehicle and began patrolling on his own. While there are many stretches of isolated road, where just about anything could happen, he always felt confident that he would be able to handle any situation." You just have to be constantly in a state of preparedness," he said.

In January 1996, Morgan was involved in the capture of Maxwell White, a man from the Reynoldsburg area, who had shot his mother and then fled the scene. When a state police officer stopped him for a minor traffic violation, White panicked and wounded the officer before taking off down the highway. Morgan was stationed at Medina at the time and working the midnight shift when he heard the news about the officer who was shot. He headed out into the cold, rainy night with three rookie officers in tow, determined to stop White from hurting anyone else. The State Highway Patrol soon received information from a couple who witnessed the shooting and were following White through the Ashland–Medina area. Authorities began a high-speed pursuit that ultimately ended with White losing control of his vehicle and hitting a culvert as he attempted to exit to State Road 18. Morgan, who was at the scene when White crashed, said, "He was ready to shoot it out but fortunately he lost his weapon in the crash."

Morgan also participated in the investigation into the death of Dr. Gulam Moonda, sixty-nine, in May 2005. The Moondas of Hermitage, Pennsylvania, had been visiting relatives in Ohio when his forty-six-year-old wife Donna, who was driving, stopped their car by the side of the Ohio Turnpike near Cleveland. Although Donna said that Moonda had been fatally wounded by a man who appeared out of nowhere and robbed them, authorities became suspicious when they discovered that only the doctor's valuables were missing. The State Highway Patrol soon discovered that Donna, who had signed a prenuptial agreement, would have only received $250,000, if she divorced her husband. With Moonda dead, she stood to inherit about $3 million plus $676,000 in insurance premiums. The police learned that she had allegedly arranged her husband's murder with her boyfriend, Damien Bradford of Aliquippa, Pennsylvania.

Donna and Damien had apparently met while she was a patient at a drug rehabilitation center in Pennsylvania. She had developed an addiction while working as a nurse anesthetist at a local hospital and had stolen fentynal from the hospital. Morgan noted that Damien, like many amateur criminals, never realized that his cell phone conversations with Donna on the night of the murder helped the State Patrol trace his movements to the scene of the crime.

But like many dedicated officers, Morgan is still haunted by a case that occurred in July 2003, when he was stationed in Cleveland as head of the investigative section there. That was when California police captured Manuel Gehring, a man who had abducted

CRIME BY THE NUMBERS

According to statistics provided by the Ohio Department of Public Safety, while the Buckeye State's population increased just slightly between 1994 and 2004 from about 11.1 to 11.4 million, reported incidents of violent crime have actually gone down. In 1994, 53,930 crimes were reported, including 662 murders, 5,231 rapes, 20,821 robberies, and 27,216 assaults. Ten years later, those numbers had dropped to 45,124 reported incidents, including 517 murders, 4,646 rapes, 17,543 robberies, and 16,457 assaults. According to Crime State Rankings 2008, Ohio is listed at number 29 out of 50 in its Safe State Ranking.

his two children during a Fourth of July celebration in Concord, New Hampshire. Gehring, involved in a custody dispute with his ex-wife Theresa Knight, admitted that he had shot and killed Philip, age eleven, and Sarah, age fourteen, while they were traveling west and that he had buried their bodies at an unknown location off of a turnpike exit near Akron. Since he could not remember the exact location, both state and municipal police officers repeatedly scoured the region without success for any signs of the two graves that Gehring said he had marked with two wooden crosses.

"For eight months after that, I would take my family for a ride through the area each Sunday after we got out of church," Morgan said. "Unfortunately, we never discovered where the children were buried."

In December 2005, two-and-a-half years after the children were murdered, a trainer from Texas and her cadaver dog, as such specially trained animals are known, found Philip and Sarah's graves near Interstate 80, off of a service road near an oil well in Hudson, just about six miles from Morgan's home. Charged with two counts of murder, Gehring committed suicide while in custody at the Merrimack County Jail in Boscawen, New Hampshire, before his case went to trial. Although such cases still evoke painful memories, Morgan believed that he ultimately made the right career choice for himself all those years ago.

Long before the creation of a state or municipal police force, Ohio residents relied on the sheriff and his deputies to maintain law and order. During the region's earliest years of settlement, the sheriff was appointed by the colonial governor. According to www.buckeyesheriffs.com, the first man to hold that post was Col. Ebenezer Sproat, whose jurisdiction included all of Washington County after he was appointed in 1788.

After Ohio became a state in 1803, the sheriff was elected by the voters and they chose William Skinner for the job. But then, as now, law enforcement was not always able to keep up with the growing population and its ever-increasing criminal element. By the end of the nineteenth century, Ohio had been transformed from an agricultural state to an industrial one, where thousands of people flocked in search of jobs. Within a few short years, the state's population doubled to more than four million people who worked as coal and iron ore miners, in the oil business, in rubber and steel manufacturing, and later in the automobile plants that opened in Ohio. In those early days, the sheriff's job was often complicated by residents who took the law into their own hands.

These days, county sheriffs serve four-year terms, and in all of Ohio's eighty-eight counties, they are considered the chief law enforcement officers. Not only do they maintain full police power in all townships and municipalities, but they are responsible for providing court services, running the jails, and extraditing and transporting prisoners.

Like their colleagues on the Ohio State Highway Patrol, municipal police officers are regularly confronted by drunken drivers and thieves, but they also deal with domestic disputes and other crimes unique to community life.

Columbus, the capital of Ohio and the largest city in the state, was founded in 1812 on the banks of the Scioto and Olentangy rivers. Its prime location on the water soon made it an industrial center, but growth and development also attracted its share of crime. Today, the city of more than 750,000 ranks at number fifty-five on the list of top hundred cities where murders occur. The chances of being a victim there of a violent crime, such as assault, are also more than double that of the rest of the state—8.3 compared to 3.5—according to www.neighborhoodscout.com. It is interesting to note that despite the size of its population, its police department today only numbers about seventy-eight officers.

Columbus was first patrolled in the late 1800s by City Marshal Pat Hagerty, who was assisted by Deputy George Lewellen. By 1895, the city started a small police force that consisted of eight men: John Ferguson, Newton Clark, George Smith, Roger Dixon, Ed Garrison, Dan Hoffman, Henry Hoffman, and Jim Henry. Using the offices of a local newspaper as their headquarters, they worked twelve-hour shifts and patrolled with four men on duty at a time.

By 1910, Columbus city officials appointed Stanley Cooper as the first chief of police and built the first police department. Cooper supervised eight officers, who received a salary of about $50 a month. Like their descendants, they dealt with theft, assault, vandalism, and on occasion, murder. In 1930, the Columbus Police Department paid $700 for its first patrol car—a Pontiac convertible equipped with a slot for a machine gun, as well as a bulletproof windshield and side shields. At that time, notorious bank robbers like John Dillinger were rampaging through the Midwest and they didn't hesitate to shoot at the police. Nine years later, the department acquired a new transmitter that allowed each police station to communicate directly with the patrol cars. Today, the police have about fifty cars that are equipped with everything from laptop computers to video cameras. The Columbus police, like those in other major cities and small towns throughout the Buckeye State, deal on a daily basis with a variety of crimes that can sometimes have fatal results.

According to the Ohio Department of Public Safety, two Ohio State Highway Patrol officers were killed in the line of duty in 2007. That same year, a Toledo police detective with thirteen years of experience was shot and killed by a fifteen-year-old suspect while working undercover on a drug operation. In Cleveland Heights, a seven-year veteran of the police department was fatally wounded after responding to the scene of a large fight. In addition, 144 different Ohio agencies reported 472 assaults on police officers during 2007; eighty-four percent of those assaults were committed with some type of weapon, and two percent were committed with a firearm. Yet despite these ominous statistics, the rate of assault per one hundred officers in Ohio that year was 7.8, which was below the 11.4 per one hundred officers for the rest of the United States.

While many of their assailants were immediately brought to justice, more than forty years passed before his fellow officers could close the case of Patrolman Donald Martin, badge number P338, of the Cincinnati Police Department. Martin, who served between 1956 and 1961, lived at 4300 Foley Road with his wife Gail. A veteran of the Korean War who had received three Bronze Stars, he was twenty-nine when he was shot by someone who managed to grab his service revolver after a struggle in the parking lot of the National Biscuit Company (Nabisco) at 721 Reading Road.

It was at about three o'clock on the morning of March 11, 1961, when Martin pulled his patrol car into the parking lot next door to the Downtown Lincoln Mercury car lot at 715 Reading Road. He left his vehicle after he saw Walter Walls and Jesse Walls steal a battery from one of the cars while Charles Jillson waited for them in a nearby car. During a confrontation, Walter Walls grabbed Martin's .38-caliber service revolver and shot the officer in the chest and in the back when he attempted to run from the scene. After Martin fell, Walls fired a final round into the officer's head. Three witnesses, Hugh Moore, Harold Stiver, and Jack Wenner, were on their way home from a night of gambling in Kentucky when they passed the car lot and saw Walls fire the final, fatal shot.

As Jillson drove off, Jesse Walls fled east through the Nabisco parking lot toward the railroad tracks. Walls raced across Reading Road and ran up a muddy embankment on Dandridge Street, where he discarded Martin's gun and his shirt and jacket in a nearby trash can. In the meantime, the witnesses tried to assist the wounded officer. While Stiver remained with Martin, Moore and Wenner drove to a gas station to call the police. Armed with a description of Martin's killer, the police scoured the neighborhood and found the officer's revolver and Walls's shirt and jacket. With no further information forthcoming, however, the police were unable to make an arrest. Martin would eventually become a cold case that was periodically reviewed during the next forty years.

According to John Boertlein, author of *Ohio Confidential*, detectives Jeff Schare and Kurt Ballman "happened to be on duty in February 2005 when a small, fragile-looking woman came to the homicide squad at Criminal Investigation Section headquarters at

824 Broadway with a disturbing story." The woman told the detectives that her former husband, Walter Walls, had admitted to killing Martin more than forty years before. But when he proved to be a violent, abusive alcoholic, she was too afraid to step forward and tell authorities what she knew.

Intrigued by her story, the detectives decided to examine the case once again. They learned that Walls's children knew about the murder, but were also too afraid to tell the police. It wasn't until Walls died in 2004 that family members felt they could safely tell the story. As a result, the murder of Patrolman Donald Martin was officially closed because his killer was dead. Martin's name is one of hundreds inscribed on the walls at the Ohio Fallen Officers' Memorial, located at the Ohio Peace Officer Training Academy in London.

Despite the dangers of the job, Ohio's state and municipal police departments, together with sheriff's officers and other law enforcement agencies work hard to keep a lid on crime. In 2004, there were 351,879 Ohio residents either in jail or on parole, a figure that was twenty-seven percent higher than the national average. While some were easier to convict than others, there were, of course, the unexpected moments that undoubtedly were very gratifying. In March 2010, the Associated Press reported that a motorist, attempting to escape from police in Cleveland, jumped out of his vehicle and over a fence only to find himself in the yard of the state women's prison. The driver, who had led authorities on a high-speed chase after being cited for a traffic violation, was promptly arrested along with two other passengers who also had tried to flee from the police.

Epilogue

These stories are just a small sampling of the many different types of crimes that have occurred in Ohio since European settlers arrived there in the seventeenth century. Over the years, the Buckeye State has seen its share of murderers and thieves, as well as crooked politicians like Gov. James Rhodes, psychopathic personalities such as Charles Manson, and even traitors like Mildred Gillars, better known during World War II as "Axis Sally."

There are many different theories about why people commit crimes, ranging from abuse during childhood to the idea that some are just plain born evil. But it's highly unlikely that anyone will ever be able to completely understand what motivates someone to hurt another person. Take, for example, the case of Bobby Lee Cutts Jr., a former Canton police officer who was sentenced in 2007 to fifty-seven years to life for killing his pregnant girlfriend, Jessie Davis, and their unborn child at Davis's home in Stark County. Although family members found the couple's young son in the house, Davis was missing for nine days before her body was discovered dumped in a park. Cutts at first told authorities he had no idea of Davis's whereabouts, and then later admitted killing her. He said that her death was an accident that had occurred during an argument, but prosecutors declared Cutts killed her to avoid making additional child support payments. Although his attorney presented numerous appeals to the courts, the Ohio Supreme Court rejected yet another effort on his behalf in 2009. It is unlikely that Cutts will be released from prison before serving at least the minimum term. And it is even less likely that anyone will ever know if the motive behind Cutts's actions was money or something that perhaps he has not even acknowledged to himself.

Then, in October 2009, Cleveland authorities arrested fifty-year-old Anthony Sowell, a registered sex offender, after they discovered the bodies of eleven women at his three-story home on the east side of the city. Although he pleaded not guilty by reason of insanity to multiple counts of murder, attempted murder, rape, assault, and kidnapping, Cuyahoga County Prosecutor Bill Mason planned in early 2010 to seek the death penalty.

Sowell had previously served fifteen years in prison on charges of attempted rape before being released in 2005. In April 2009, a woman reported that after she partied with him for an afternoon, Sowell attacked her. When another similar incident occurred that September involving a different woman, the police arrived at his home armed with a warrant for his arrest. That was when they discovered the first of the bodies. After authorities returned with a search warrant, the number soon climbed to eleven badly decomposed corpses found inside and buried in shallow graves behind the house. According to www.cnn.com, "Most of the women whose remains were found were strangled by ligature—which could include a string, cord, or wire—and at least one was strangled by hand, officials said." The Cleveland police reviewed cold case files to see if Sowell may have been involved in some other unsolved murders in the city, and the Associated Press reported in 2010 that the FBI was examining unsolved murders and incidents of assault that occurred in California, North Carolina, South Carolina, and Japan, where Sowell was stationed as a Marine between 1978 and 1985.

Even though it's unlikely that we'll ever know why some people choose to break the law while the rest prefer to live responsibly, it should make most Ohio residents feel better to know that the "bad guys" are still in the minority. The Buckeye State may no longer be one of the safest places to live in America, but it still has a lot of positive assets that strongly outweigh the negatives. So make that trip into Cleveland to visit the Rock and Roll Hall of Fame and Museum. Or head to Dennison to enjoy the annual Railroad Festival that has been a staple of the community for more than thirty years. Just remember, like Americans everywhere, to make sure that at the end of the day you've locked the doors.

Bibliography

Books

Bellamy, John Stark II. *The Killer in the Attic and More True Tales of Crime and Disaster from Cleveland's Past.* Cleveland: Gray, 2002.

Boertlein, John. *Ohio Confidential: Sex, Scandal, Murder, and Mayhem in the Buckeye State.* Cincinnati: Clerisy Press, 2008.

Cox, Bill G., et al. *Crimes of the 20th Century: A Chronology.* Lincolnwood, IL: Crescent Books, 1991.

Edwards, Ed. *Metamorphosis of a Criminal.* New York: Hart Publishing, 1972.

Fornshell, Marvin E. *The Historical and Illustrated Ohio Penitentiary.* 1907–08.

Franklin, Diana Britt. *The Good-Bye Door: The Incredible True Story of America's First Female Serial Killer to Die in the Chair.* Kent, OH: Kent State University Press, 2006.

Friedman, Lawrence M. *Crime and Punishment in American History.* New York: BasicBooks, 1993.

Gindy, Gaye E. *Murder in Sylvania, Ohio as Told in 1857.* Bloomington, IN: AuthorHouse, 2007.

Greenberg, Keith Elliot, and Vincent Felber. *Perfect Beauty: A True Story of Adultery, Murder, and Manipulation in Middle America.* New York: St. Martin's Press, 2008.

Howe, Henry. *Historical Collections of Ohio in Two Volumes: An Encyclopedia of the State.* Norwalk, OH: Laning Printing, 1898.

Moldea, Dan E. *The Hoffa Wars: The Rise and Fall of Jimmy Hoffa.* New York: S.P.I. Books, 1992.

Monkkonen, Eric H. *The Dangerous Class: Crime and Poverty in Columbus, Ohio, 1860–1885.* Cambridge, MA: Harvard University Press, 1975.

Morgan, Kathleen O'Leary, and Scott Morgan, eds. *Crime State Rankings 2008.* Washington, DC: CQ Press, 2008.

Neff, James. *The Wrong Man: The Final Verdict on the Dr. Sam Sheppard Murder Case.* New York: Random House, 2001.

Nickel, Steven. *Torso: The Story of Eliot Ness and the Search for a Psychopathic Killer.* Winston-Salem, NC: John F. Blair, 1989.

Slingerland, William Henry. *Child Welfare Work in Pennsylvania: A Co-Operative Study of Child Welfare Agencies and Institutions.* 1915; reprint, Ithaca, NY: Cornell University Library, 2009.

Stille, Darlene R. *Ohio.* New York: Scholastic, 2009.

Streib, Victor L. *The Fairer Death: Executing Women in Ohio.* Athens, OH: Ohio University Press, 2006.

Online Sources

Associated Press. "Cleveland Man Indicted on 11 Counts of Murder." *Canton Repository.* Retrieved January 23, 2010. www.cantonrep.com/archive/x1792918848/Cleveland-man-indicted-on-11-counts-of-murder.

"Cleveland Bosses." *Cleveland Mob.* Retrieved December 1, 2009. www.clevelandmob.com/bosses.html.

Corderi, Victoria. "Dangerous Liaisons." *MSNBC.* Retrieved January 12, 2010. www.msnbc.msn.com/id/18554869.

"Crime in Cincinnati." *Ohio Crime.* Retrieved October 12, 2009. www.crimestats.ohio.gov/cincinnati.

"Death Row Inmates." *Ohio Department of Rehabilitation and Correction.* Retrieved February 14, 2010. www.drc.ohio.gov/Public/deathrow.htm.

"Department History." *Columbus Police Department.* Retrieved February 19, 2010. www.columbuspd.com/history.html.

"Ex-Fugitive Held in 1980 Slayings." *Newslibrary.* Retrieved October 15, 2009. www.nl.newsbank.com/nl.search/we/Archives.

Greenburg, Zack O'Malley. "America's Safest Cities." *Forbes.* Retrieved February 20, 2010. www.forbes.com/2009/10/26/safest-cities-ten-lifestyle-real-estate-metros-msa.html.

Gustafson, Leona. "Ohio: The Buckeye State." *The American Local History Network.* Retrieved September 4, 2009. www.genealogybug.net/ohio-alhn/ohio.htm.

"History of the Sheriff." *Buckeye State Sheriff's Association.* Retrieved February 17, 2010. www.buckeyesheriffs.org/history.html.

Kernene-Prisbrey, Bonnie. "This Day in Crime History." *Bonnie's Blog of Crime.* Retrieved November 7, 2009. www.mylifeofcrime.wordpress.com/category-ohio.

McGunagle, Fred. "Sam Sheppard." *TruTV Library.* Retrieved December 14, 2009. www.truetv.com/library/crime/notorious-murders/famous/sheppard/index-1.html.

"Ohio History Timeline." *e-Reference Desk*. Retrieved November 14, 2009. www.e-referencedesk.com/resources/state-history-timeline/ohio.htm.

"Ohio Penitentiary." *Ohio History Central*. Retrieved November 7, 2009. www.ohiohistorycentral.org/entry.php?rec=783.

"Ohio's Fallen Officers." *Ohio's Fallen Officers*. Retrieved February 18, 2010. www.ohiofallenofficers.com.

"Patrol's Memorial." *Ohio Department of Public Safety*. Retrieved February 22, 2010. www.statepatrol.ohio.gov/memory.stm.

Porello, Rick. "The Cleveland La Cosa Nostra." *American Mafia*. Retrieved December 13, 2009. www.americanmafia.com/Cities/Cleveland.html.

"Sam Sheppard's Remains Exhumed for DNA Testing." *CNN*. Retrieved October 3, 2009. www.cnn.com/US/9709/17/sheppard/index.html?iref =allsearch.

"Statistics for the State of Ohio." *National Institute of Corrections*. Retrieved February 16, 2010. www.nicic.org/Features/StateStats/Default .aspx?State=OH.

"Timothy Hack & Kelly Drew." *Crime News 2000*. Retrieved March 30, 2010. www.crimenews2000.com/comment.php?comment.news.1266.

"Weather: What Is the Century's Worst In Ohio?" *WEWS Newsnet5.com*. Retrieved October 29, 2009. www.weathernet5.com/dpp/weather/ Weather:What-Is-The-Century's-Worst-in-Ohio?.

Acknowledgments

I am grateful to the following people for their invaluable assistance in creating this book: my editor, Kyle Weaver; assistant editor Brett Keener; Lisa Long of the Ohio Historical Society; Corey Kregenow, assistant curator for the Cleveland Police Museum and Historical Society; staff lieutenant Monte Morgan of the Ohio State Highway Patrol; and of course, the staff of the Vineland Public Library.

Other Titles in the
True Crime Series